OPPOSING VIEWPOINTS® SERIES

Gay Parenting

Other Books of Related Interest:

"Congress shall make
no law . . . abridging
the freedom of speech,
or of the press."

First Amendment to the US Constitution

The basic foundation of our democracy is the First Amendment guarantee of freedom of expression. The Opposing Viewpoints series is dedicated to the concept of this basic freedom and the idea that it is more important to practice it than to enshrine it.

OPPOSING VIEWPOINTS® SERIES

| Gay Parenting

Beth Rosenthal, Book Editor

GREENHAVEN PRESS
A part of Gale, Cengage Learning

GALE
CENGAGE Learning·

Detroit • New York • San Francisco • New Haven, Conn • Waterville, Maine • London

Elizabeth Des Chenes, *Director, Publishing Solutions*

© 2013 Greenhaven Press, a part of Gale, Cengage Learning.

Gale and Greenhaven Press are registered trademarks used herein under license.

For more information, contact:
Greenhaven Press
27500 Drake Rd.
Farmington Hills, MI 48331-3535
Or you can visit our Internet site at gale.cengage.com

For product information and technology assistance, contact us at

Gale Customer Support, 1-800-877-4253
For permission to use material from this text or product, submit all requests online at www.cengage.com/permissions

Further permissions questions can be emailed to permissionrequest@cengage.com

Articles in Greenhaven Press anthologies are often edited for length to meet page requirements. In addition, original titles of these works are changed to clearly present the main thesis and to explicitly indicate the author's opinion. Every effort is made to ensure that Greenhaven Press accurately reflects the original intent of the authors. Every effort has been made to trace the owners of copyrighted material.

Cover Image copyright © Nick Cardillicchio/Corbis.

LIBRARY OF CONGRESS CATALOGING-IN-PUBLICATION DATA

Gay parenting / Beth Rosenthal, book editor.
    p. cm. -- (Opposing viewpoints)
    Includes bibliographical references and index.
    ISBN 978-0-7377-6422-2 (hardcover) -- ISBN 978-0-7377-6423-9 (pbk.)
    1. Gay parents. 2. Parenting. 3. Families. I. Rosenthal, Beth, 1964-
    HQ75.27.G397 2012
    306.874086'64--dc23
                                                    2012016629

Contents

Chapter 3: What Methods of Parenthood Should Be Available to Gays and Lesbians?

Chapter 4: What Laws Should Regulate Gay Parenting?

Why Consider Opposing Viewpoints?

> *"The only way in which a human being can make some approach to knowing the whole of a subject is by hearing what can be said about it by persons of every variety of opinion and studying all modes in which it can be looked at by every character of mind. No wise man ever acquired his wisdom in any mode but this."*
>
> *John Stuart Mill*

In our media-intensive culture it is not difficult to find differing opinions. Thousands of newspapers and magazines and dozens of radio and television talk shows resound with differing points of view. The difficulty lies in deciding which opinion to agree with and which "experts" seem the most credible. The more inundated we become with differing opinions and claims, the more essential it is to hone critical reading and thinking skills to evaluate these ideas. Opposing Viewpoints books address this problem directly by presenting stimulating debates that can be used to enhance and teach these skills. The varied opinions contained in each book examine many different aspects of a single issue. While examining these conveniently edited opposing views, readers can develop critical thinking skills such as the ability to compare and contrast authors' credibility, facts, argumentation styles, use of persuasive techniques, and other stylistic tools. In short, the Opposing Viewpoints Series is an ideal way to attain the higher-level thinking and reading skills so essential in a culture of diverse and contradictory opinions.

In addition to providing a tool for critical thinking, Opposing Viewpoints books challenge readers to question their own strongly held opinions and assumptions. Most people form their opinions on the basis of upbringing, peer pressure, and personal, cultural, or professional bias. By reading carefully balanced opposing views, readers must directly confront new ideas as well as the opinions of those with whom they disagree. This is not to argue simplistically that everyone who reads opposing views will—or should—change his or her opinion. Instead, the series enhances readers' understanding of their own views by encouraging confrontation with opposing ideas. Careful examination of others' views can lead to the readers' understanding of the logical inconsistencies in their own opinions, perspective on why they hold an opinion, and the consideration of the possibility that their opinion requires further evaluation.

Evaluating Other Opinions

To ensure that this type of examination occurs, Opposing Viewpoints books present all types of opinions. Prominent spokespeople on different sides of each issue as well as well-known professionals from many disciplines challenge the reader. An additional goal of the series is to provide a forum for other, less known, or even unpopular viewpoints. The opinion of an ordinary person who has had to make the decision to cut off life support from a terminally ill relative, for example, may be just as valuable and provide just as much insight as a medical ethicist's professional opinion. The editors have two additional purposes in including these less known views. One, the editors encourage readers to respect others' opinions—even when not enhanced by professional credibility. It is only by reading or listening to and objectively evaluating others' ideas that one can determine whether they are worthy of consideration. Two, the inclusion of such viewpoints encourages the important critical thinking skill of objectively evaluating an author's credentials and bias. This evaluation will illuminate an author's reasons for taking a particular stance on an issue and will aid in readers' evaluation of the author's ideas.

It is our hope that these books will give readers a deeper understanding of the issues debated and an appreciation of the complexity of even seemingly simple issues when good and honest people disagree. This awareness is particularly important in a democratic society such as ours in which people enter into public debate to determine the common good. Those with whom one disagrees should not be regarded as enemies but rather as people whose views deserve careful examination and may shed light on one's own.

Thomas Jefferson once said that "difference of opinion leads to inquiry, and inquiry to truth." Jefferson, a broadly educated man, argued that "if a nation expects to be ignorant and free . . . it expects what never was and never will be." As individuals and as a nation, it is imperative that we consider the opinions of others and examine them with skill and discernment. The Opposing Viewpoints series is intended to help readers achieve this goal.

David L. Bender and Bruno Leone,
Founders

Introduction

> *"A family consists of two or more people (one of whom is the householder) related by birth, marriage, or adoption residing in the same housing unit. A household consists of all people who occupy a housing unit regardless of relationship. A household may consist of a person living alone or multiple unrelated individuals or families living together."*
>
> — US Census Bureau

While the debate over the role of gay parents grows and shows no sign of abating, the structure of the traditional family has changed in many ways. A household consisting of a mother, a father, and children living in one home has changed. According to "America's Families and Living Arrangements"—a November 3, 2011, report released by the US Census Bureau—in 2011, 69 percent of the 74.6 million children under the age of eighteen lived with two parents (92 percent of these children lived with two biological or two adoptive parents), while 27 percent lived with one parent, and 4 percent with no parents. The majority (87%) of those children who lived with only one parent lived with their mother. Fewer Americans are marrying in general, according to a December 2011 poll by the Pew Research Center. Fifty-one percent of Americans eighteen and older are married; this is a decrease from the 72 percent of Americans eighteen and older who were married in 1960.

Now as more and more same-sex couples want to become parents—and are able to become parents as a result of adoption or assisted reproductive technologies—the image of what commonly has been viewed as traditional family structure continues to blur. Americans are torn about the changes: A February 2011 survey by the Pew Research Center found that Americans are divided about the effects that such trends as same-sex couples raising children have on society.

Those who oppose the idea of gay, lesbian, bisexual, and transgender people having and raising children argue that the traditional family structure serves as the basis for society, and without it, society as a whole will deteriorate and suffer. Collette Caprara in a Heritage Foundation blog entry, entitled "Reinventing the Family: Good Intentions Are Not Enough," on October 24, 2011, writes:

> Youths growing up with both a mother and father in the home are also less likely to engage in high-risk behaviors such as becoming sexually active or engaging in substance abuse and less likely to exhibit antisocial behavior. In addition, teens in intact families tend to fare better on a range of emotional and psychological outcomes and to have higher levels of academic achievement and educational attainment. With an apparent disregard for the social and economic consequences to children, the rise of experimental family forms and the "commissioning" of babies may be the ultimate expression of the commodification of children—when offspring are conceived for the gratification of adults who have yet to grow up.

Supporters of same-sex parents maintain their desire to create families—even through such nonconventional methods as assisted reproductive technology and surrogacy—is no different from the desire of heterosexuals who wish to raise a family. In "Meet My Real Modern Family" in the January 30, 2011, issue of *Newsweek*, Andrew Solomon discusses his relationship with his husband (they had a civil-partnership ceremony in England and were married in Connecticut) and their four children. Solomon is the biological father to a friend's daughter, with whom he has a relationship, while his husband, John, has a relationship with the two children he fathered for friends of his. Solomon and John have a child together with the help of a surrogate mother and in vitro fertilization (IVF). Solomon realizes that people accept his brother's traditional family without question, while his own family often is questioned—even though he and John love each other and their four children. He writes, "All happy families are the same, and yet, when my brother says he loves his wife and children, everyone is delighted; when I speak of loving my family, people are often shocked and occasionally disgusted. Our affection becomes political—thrilling in a way, but I'd prefer to have intimacy untainted by purpose. That photo on the iPhone [a picture of Solomon, John, and their four children that was taken on the day that he and John were married in Connecticut and had the naming ceremony for their son] often seems euphemistic, because what it shows looks easy. It is exhilarating to be Christopher Columbus landing on the wilder shores of love, but sometimes one would prefer to live where the luxury hotels have already been built and Internet access is wireless."

Opposing Viewpoints: Gay Parenting explores the continuing debate over the effect that gay, lesbian, bisexual, and transgender parents have on their children in particular, as well as on society as a whole. The topics covered include the impact of gay parenting on children, the impact of gay families on society, the methods of parenthood available to gays and lesbians, and what laws should regulate gay parenting. The viewpoints presented in this volume examine how same-sex parents and their children can be accepted as simply another type of family to some, while representing a breakdown of society to others.

OPPOSING
VIEWPOINTS®
SERIES

CHAPTER 1

What Is the Impact of Gay Parenting on Children?

Chapter Preface

Approximately 250,000 children under the age of eighteen were being raised by approximately 116,000 same-sex couples in the United States in 2008, according to US census data analyzed by demographer Gary J. Gates, a scholar at the Williams Institute. The 2000 census had reported that there were approximately 63,000 same-sex couples in the United States bringing up children.

The debate over how lesbian, gay, bisexual, and transgender (LGBT) couples affect their children rages even as these numbers climb. Opponents of permitting gays and lesbians to become adoptive parents maintain that the most appropriate homes for children are those with a mother and a father. In a November 2, 2011, interview with the American Family News Network, Janice Crouse of Concerned Women for America said, "Something around 65,000 adopted children and 14,000 foster children live in homes that are headed by nonheterosexuals, and yet the data very overwhelmingly says these homes are not as good for children. They don't even come close to being as good for children as a married couple—mom and dad—family."

Not allowing gays and lesbians to adopt only hurts children who need stable homes, argue supporters of gay-parent adoption. A blogger on the website of People for the American Way wrote on February 21, 2012, that "successful parenting is not dependent on sexual orientation or gender identity. Laws and policies that discriminate against otherwise qualified LGBT parents are failing the half million children in the foster care system, 120,000 of whom are eligible for adoption. We should be giving these children more places to turn, instead of needlessly and cruelly closing the door to safe, loving homes. They deserve care and permanency with their best interests at heart, not placements that forsake them for ideology or political gain."

The 2010 census gave gays and lesbians the opportunity to check themselves off as "married" for the first time in the history of the US census. Supporters of gay and lesbian families argue that counting the number of same-sex couples and their children is important because it highlights the continuing discrimination that gays and lesbians and their families face in their everyday lives. On September 27, 2011, the Human Rights Campaign announced that "elected officials at all levels cannot continue to pretend that laws discriminating against our community aren't harming real families, families who live in their cities, counties, districts and states. These new census numbers provide advocacy groups and LGBT individuals a powerful tool in demanding our equality."

Those who oppose gay parenting counter that the federal government is legitimizing a lifestyle that they feel is offensive and harmful to children and undermines society as a whole. In an April 8, 2010, *New American* article, entitled "Census Bureau Encouraging Homosexual Couples to Identify as 'Married,'" Peter LaBarbera of Americans for Truth About Homosexuality states, "There was a time when homosexual activists just lied and said that ten percent of the public was gay. . . . It took decades to disprove that lie, but here again we see them calling themselves married because they want to be called married. Well, that's not what the law says."

As the number of gay and lesbian couples who have children increases, so do the arguments over the effects and impact that lesbian, gay, bisexual, and transgender parents have on their children. The authors of the viewpoints in the following chapter debate whether or not these children have more problems than their peers who have heterosexual parents, whether a family must include a mother and father in order to be considered a family, gay custody cases, and how—if at all—the definition of parenthood should be revised.

"Heterosexual couples . . . provide society with children who have two biological parents, usually coupled with each other. Same-sex couples may have only children with at most one biological parent in the pair."

Children of Lesbian and Gay Parents Are More Likely to Have Problems

Walter Schumm, as told to LifeSiteNews.com

In the following viewpoint, Walter Schumm, in an interview with LifeSiteNews.com, maintains that gay and lesbian parents are unable to offer their children a stable family structure, and as a result, their children are more likely to suffer from emotional and social problems. He argues that recent studies do not accurately reflect these issues because many researchers are too concerned about being perceived as homophobic. Schumm contends that only a man and woman are best able to provide the secure and settled environment that children need to thrive. Schumm is a professor of family studies and human services at Kansas State University. LifeSiteNews.com is a non-profit Internet service dedicated to issues of culture, life, and family.

As you read, consider the following questions:

1. In Schumm's opinion, why are some researchers worried about being seen as homophobic?

2. According to Schumm, why were his and Dr. George Rekers's testimonies attacked as not being credible?

3. In Schumm's opinion, how is the judiciary establishing "a great inequality" in the way in which it is treating same-sex and heterosexual relationships?

Judge [Vaughn] Walker built his decision [on August 4, 2010] overturning Proposition 8 [an amendment to the California constitution passed in November 2008 that bans same-sex marriages in that state] on many "findings of fact," which to a great extent came from experts supplied by the opponents of Proposition 8. But according to Dr. Walter Schumm, professor of family studies and human services at Kansas State University, many of these so-called facts are either false or doubtful.

In the following interview with LifeSiteNews.com (LSN), Dr. Schumm explains that homosexual parents are more likely to raise homosexual children; that scholars are often biased in favor of research friendly to the homosexual agenda; and that legalizing homosexual "marriage" places an unjust burden upon heterosexual families.

Children Are Influenced by Their Parents' Sexual Orientation

LSN: The 71st finding of fact in Judge Walker's decision states that children "raised by gay or lesbian parents are as likely as children raised by heterosexual parents to be healthy, successful, and well adjusted." What does your research show about the influence of homosexual parents on their children, especially in terms of sexual orientation?

Dr. Schumm: For decades it was politically correct to argue that parental sexual orientation had nothing to do with a child's sexual orientation. However, about 1995 or so, a few scholars began to admit that, at least in theory, parental values would be expected to influence children's values, including sexual orientation preferences. Nevertheless, it was argued that even such an expected result had little empirical support. I decided to tackle this difficult problem from three perspectives, in a report in press with the Cambridge journal *Journal of Biosocial Science* [published in November 2010].

First, I reviewed ten books concerning over 250 children of gay, lesbian, or bisexual [GLB] parents and valuated the children's own stories about their sexual orientations. I used a 10% baseline for a simulated comparison group of heterosexual families. It was clear that the children of GLB parents were more likely to either have identified as GLB or to have at least experimented with nonheterosexual behavior. The more I controlled for age (using older children) and availability of data (using only those children who specifically described their sexual orientations), the stronger the results became. Gender was an interesting and strong factor in that the daughters of lesbian mothers were most likely to reject a heterosexual orientation whereas sons of gay fathers were least likely to do so.

I then compiled data from 26 studies about GLB parenting and found that children of GLB parents were more likely to report a nonheterosexual orientation than were children of heterosexual parents in those studies, an effect that was strongest for mothers.

Third, I studied reports from a number of cultures from around the world and found that the less strongly those cultures condemned homosexuality, the less rare was its actual (open) practice.

Thus, all three sources of data indicate that sexual orientation, at least in terms of its open expression, is subject to the influence of social and cultural factors, including family background. While not surprising in terms of what social science theory might predict, the results differ greatly from the testimony of many experts at a host of previous court cases concerning gay or lesbian parenting.

Gay and Lesbian Parents Do Not Want Their Child to Be Heterosexual

Furthermore, my analysis of previous data, some of which has seldom been mentioned, showed that gay or lesbian parents were less likely to want their children to grow up to be heterosexual than were heterosexual parents. Gay and lesbian parents also seemed less likely to expect that their children would grow up to be heterosexual. Thus, both parental expectations and aspirations tend to pressure children to model their parents' own sexual orientation, providing a clear pathway for parental sexual orientation to influence a child's sexual orientation.

The media has covered studies reporting that children raised by homosexual parents do as well as or even better than children raised by heterosexual parents. Has media coverage of these stories been accurate? Are there any flaws in such studies that have been overlooked?

The problem of determining how parental sexual orientation might influence a child's health or psychological adjustment is more complicated than many recognize. It is becoming increasingly clear from research that lesbian mothers tend to have less stable relationships than heterosexual mothers and fathers, an issue seldom considered by researchers.

When it has been considered, it is usually found that the children of single parents do worse than children of two parents. That might not sound like much, but the issue is that if lesbian mothers are less likely to remain in a two-parent structure, merely comparing single lesbian parents with (heterosexual) single parents buries the adverse risks of lesbian parenting in the single-parent issue, essentially obscuring the risks to children of parental breakups. If the scientific models predicted child outcomes from parental stability and predicted parental stability from parental sexual orientation, we might observe some important adverse indirect effects of parental sexual orientation.

Likewise, I have yet to see a study which has monitored outcomes such as sexual compulsivity or general delayed gratification (also known as time preference) among children of the various types of parents. Some research that has looked at abuse of drugs or insecure attachment has found strongly adverse results for daughters of gay fathers.

Furthermore, many of the studies have set up questionable comparisons of GLB and heterosexual parents. Often, the GLB parents have higher education, higher incomes, fewer children, as well as a likely desire to present their children in a socially desirable manner for the sake of "the cause." I have yet to see any study that has controlled for or taken into account per-capita household income when comparing children from both types of households. Few studies have controlled for social desirability, especially what might be labeled "parental social desirability." One recent study used gay fathers from households earning an average of $190,000 annually, which put them easily into the top 5% of all U.S. households for income. Generalizing from the top 5% of all households to all households is simply not appropriate scientifically, even if few differences are observed across types of parents among the top 5% of households. Some studies have sampled "same-sex" parents but may have included grandmothers and mothers or mother/adult daughter pairs who are raising children, yet they expect readers to draw conclusions about the favorability of GLB parenting.

Unequal Representation of the Issues

During the case, Judge Walker ruled that the testimony of David Blankenhorn [founder of the Institute for American Values], one of the two witnesses who testified for the proponents of Proposition 8, constituted "inadmissible opinion testimony that should be given essentially no weight."

Leaving aside the question of whether Judge Walker was correct to so decide, can it [be] difficult for research that does not fit into the agenda of LGBT [lesbian, gay, bisexual, and transgender] activists to be accepted in the court, academia, or elsewhere? Could you give examples?

In my view, few scholars are willing to evaluate research on GLB parenting or marriage issues critically. There are just too many mistakes that are published, as if the peer-review process was not very effective. Some journals refuse to publish any critique of their articles, including articles dealing with GLB issues, rendering the "give and take" of academic scholarship mute.

My own research has shown that articles featuring "pro-gay" outcomes are much more likely to be cited scientifically than those featuring "anti-gay" results, even if the authors, time frame, and journals are the same. I have also found that sometimes, the worse the quality of the research in this area, the more likely it is to have been cited in major reviews of the literature.

Professors who do research in this area have to be very careful lest they offend the wrong people because even false allegations about one's being "homophobic" can lead to adverse professional evaluations, regardless of other professional criteria. If a journal is willing to publish adverse outcomes for GLB parenting it is at risk of being blackballed and deemed "unscientific"; thus, editors of journals must have tremendous courage to buck the current of political correctness and allow fair peer review of such research.

One issue that Judge Walker raised was that expert testimony could be ruled less valuable if it was based on research done for the sake of litigation. This is almost amusing. It doesn't seem to matter if pro-gay scholars do research or critiques of research as part of litigation, but it seems to matter if other scholars do so. In the Florida trial on gay adoption with which I was involved as an expert witness, at least one of the "pro-gay" experts was paid $200 an hour for 70 hours ($14,000 total) to critique my research. Clearly, this was done as part of the litigation, but that didn't seem to reduce her credibility in the eyes of the court. So, I feel there may be a double standard at work here.

In some states, like Florida, it is actually against the law to try to impeach a witness's credibility on the basis of their religious beliefs or views. Nevertheless, that didn't stop the lawyers on the pro-gay adoption side of the trial from attacking the credibility of witnesses on the basis of their religious views or affiliations—you might remember how harshly Dr. George Rekers, a Ph.D. clinical psychologist, was attacked for also being a Baptist minister, which appeared to discredit his views in the eyes of the court, as I interpreted the decision. My own testimony was raked over the coals because of a half-sentence from a much longer opinion paper in which I mentioned using science to highlight the truths of Scripture. The court overlooked the fact that I have actually tested (and published) various Scriptures and religious doctrines statistically in ways that would permit acceptance or rejection of the hypotheses involved. In other words, I was very open to findings that the Scriptures were not correct from a scientific perspective, but the statement was taken out of the larger contexts of both the particular paper and of my overall research program to imply that I would bias my research to support certain "religious" perspectives.

There Is Less Family Stability in Homosexual Relationships

The 76th finding of fact states that it is an entirely unsupported stereotype that homosexuals are "incapable of forming long-term intimate relationships." The 48th states that same-sex "couples

Children Thrive with a Mother and a Father

There simply cannot be any serious debate, based on the mass of scholarly literature available to us, about the ideal family form for children. It consists of a mother and father who are committed to one another in marriage. Children raised by their married mother and father experience lower rates of many social pathologies, including

• premarital childbearing;

• illicit drug use;

• arrest;

• health, emotional, or behavioral problems;

• poverty;

• or school failure or expulsion.

Peter Sprigg,
"The Top Ten Harms of Same-Sex 'Marriage,'"
Family Research Council, 2011.

are identical to opposite-sex couples in the characteristics relevant to the ability to form successful marital unions." What does research indicate about the fidelity within and length of typical homosexual relationships?

Back to the stability issue, one article recently admitted that there was one previous research report showing that lesbian mothers had less stable relationships than heterosexual parents. However, I have found several others that have yielded the same results. Nevertheless, many scholars continue to assert—for example, at the Prop 8 trial—that there are no differences whatsoever between heterosexual and nonhetero-sexual relationships, even in terms of stability. Researchers have also found that gay men are much more likely than heterosexual men to engage in and approve of "extramarital" sexual affairs.

A common response to this fact is a rebuttal that if both men approve of it, what's wrong with it?

What I see wrong with it is that it begins—or perhaps continues—a process whereby we have two Americas, one free and one slave. The "free" America is where you can have sex with anyone as long as it's not rape. The "slave" America is where you can only have sex with someone you marry of the opposite gender and then never again [have sex] with anyone else as long as the marriage endures.

I am not sure how long, as [President Abraham] Lincoln observed, you can have a nation endure if it remains half-free and half-slave, with such a major cultural divide. I would expect that social entropy would favor a gradual erosion of sexual values in the direction of "freedom" from marriage and gender norms. It is as if you made a national policy that half the nation would get a "free" guaranteed annual income while the other half had to earn their income and pay for the "free" income of the rest. I am not sure how long those who had to earn their income (just as some have to earn their right to sex by making a marriage commitment and by accepting the inherent conflicts involved in gender differences) would continue to put up with such a division peacefully.

Only Heterosexual Couples Can Serve as Positive Role Models

Judge Walker argues that it is simple justice to provide same-sex couples with the same rights, duties, and social recognition as opposite-sex couples. Do you think that this is the case? Why?

Judge Walker argued that it was simple justice to afford equality to same-sex couples. In my opinion, this is a case of focusing on equality of outcomes rather than taking into account equality of inputs.

For example, one might argue that all households should have "justice" in the sense of equal annual incomes and that the courts should tax households in ways that create that type of social justice.

However, doing that would overlook issues of relative risk (should those who risk their lives more often be paid the same as those who work at relatively safe desks?) and training (should those with less training be paid the same as those with more training?) and effort (should those who work less hours or who are less diligent be paid the same as those who work more hours or more diligently?).

Heterosexual or mixed-gender relationships assume risks not assumed by same-sex couples, including pregnancy caused by the other person, unwanted pregnancy, or perhaps a risk of needing an abortion. There are greater costs because only heterosexual couples accept the difficulties involved in working out gender conflicts.

There really is a "battle of the sexes" and married heterosexual couples are well aware of it. Even the gay professor Larry Kurdek has admitted this matter in an article published in the *Journal of Family Psychology* in 2008. Women are more vulnerable to injury if physically attacked by a man, so that is another heterosexual risk factor. According to [psychologist David] Keirsey, women are more likely to be feeling oriented and men truth oriented, in terms of Keirsey's personality profile, which should lead to a higher rate of personality incompatibility among mixed-gender couples. Spouses within heterosexual couples, on average, also have greater differences in level of sexual desire than do members of same-sex couples, which can also lead to numerous and intense conflicts.

Despite these greater risks and costs, heterosexual couples are important to society because only they provide society with children who have two biological parents, usually coupled with each other. Same-sex couples may have only children with at most one biological parent in the pair. I suppose this matter could be solved by allowing for polyamory [having a relationship or relationships with multiple, consenting partners] so a child might have two lesbian mothers and a biological father living as a triad, but that would take another timely court decision.

Furthermore, only heterosexual couples model for children how to manage heterosexual conflict in a constructive manner within the confines of marriage. True, heterosexual couples may not model how to manage lesbian or gay conflicts, but that omission would only matter for a small minority of children of heterosexuals who grow up to be gay, lesbian, or bisexual. By contrast, same-sex couples are not modeling how to manage heterosexual conflict for a much larger percentage of children who will grow up to be heterosexuals.

My point is that by treating unequal relationships (unequal in terms of costs and risks) as if they deserve to be equal in terms of societal benefits, the court is actually establishing a great inequality, the very opposite of what it may think it was doing.

> "*[Gay and lesbian couples are] much more likely to be tolerant, to encourage, for example, their children to play with a wider range of toys—to encourage a girl to play with both dolls and trucks.*"

Children of Lesbian and Gay Parents Are Not More Likely to Have Problems

Abbie Goldberg, as told to Suzanne Wilson

In the following viewpoint, Suzanne Wilson interviews Abbie Goldberg, who contends that the children of gay and lesbian parents do not experience more depression and stress than the children of heterosexual parents. Goldberg argues that same-sex couples are more likely to teach their children to be tolerant and to divide labor more fairly. She maintains that gay and lesbian individuals identify themselves more as parents rather than as gay or lesbian once they have children. Wilson writes for the Daily Hampshire Gazette. *Goldberg is a professor of psychology at Clark University.*

As you read, consider the following questions:

1. According to Goldberg, why is it difficult for "two gay men with a black son" to live in rural Pennsylvania?

2. In Goldberg's opinion, why does the nonbiological mother initially have more trouble adjusting to her new role as a parent?

3. According to Goldberg, why are lesbian couples less concerned about having a boy than a gay couple?

Though Abbie Goldberg's new book has an academic title—*Lesbian and Gay Parents and Their Children: Research on the Family Life Cycle*—she hopes it will find an audience among readers around the country.

Goldberg, 32, earned her doctorate in clinical psychology at the University of Massachusetts Amherst and teaches psychology at Clark University in Worcester. Goldberg says she hopes the book will be of interest to many parents—as well as to people whose work brings them into contact with same-sex couples and their children, such as judges and others in the legal world, medical professionals and school officials.

The book, which is being published by the American Psychological Association, is the first in-depth compilation and analysis of research to date on gay and lesbian parents and their families. The first of the studies she looked at were done in the 1970s; the most recent were published last year [2008]. In all, there have been more than 70, she says.

The Children of Gay and Lesbian Parents Fit into Society Well

Goldberg's own research is part of her survey. Using in-depth interviews conducted over a period of years, she has followed same-sex couples as they made the transition to parenthood. She has studied how that life-changing decision affected their relationships and their identities; she has also studied the experiences of adults raised by lesbian, gay and bisexual parents.

Goldberg says that her review of the studies clearly suggests an answer to a common question: What about the kids? Or, put more formally, how does being raised by gay or lesbian parents affect their children's well-being? The simple answer, says Goldberg, is that the children are fine.

"They're not any more likely to be depressed or stressed out," she said during a recent interview, even though a few studies show they are more apt to be teased about their families by other children. "They do just as well in school, they're just as popular, and they have just as many friends. And all the research indicates that they're very well adjusted. They're more likely to be tolerant of differences, because their parents are teaching them certain values that are positive."

Goldberg, who grew up in New York, began her college career at Brandeis University in Waltham. "I fell in love with research there," she said. A growing interest in women's mental health led her to transfer to Wesleyan University in Connecticut to work with Ruth Striegel-Moore, a professor of psychology there.

After graduating, Goldberg came to the University of Massachusetts [UMass] Amherst to pursue a doctorate in clinical psychology. Her mentor at the university was Maureen Perry-Jenkins, widely known for her own research on working-class families.

While at UMass, Goldberg did extensive research on the experiences of lesbian couples who became parents. She also spent one year at the Yale School of Medicine in New Haven, Conn., where she completed a clinical psychology internship.

Goldberg, 32, lives in Easthampton with her husband, Owen Zaret, and the couple's 7-month-old daughter, Alexandra.

In an interview last week [in July 2009], she talked about her research. What follows are edited, condensed excerpts.

[Question:] Why did you decide to write this book?

[Answer:] The key thing for people to understand is that we're in a time right now when judges and legislators are making decisions without really knowing the data. They hear from "expert" witnesses with axes to grind, who are making moral judgments. This book is for anybody who wants the facts, the data to counter morally and religiously driven arguments.

How do you know the studies are valid and not biased?

I actually discuss this in the book. I address the fact that many of these studies included small samples, less than 30 participants, which is arguably a limitation. Other studies used large samples—100-plus random participants, meaning they were not volunteers. What is key to emphasize is that these larger studies' findings were no different than those obtained in studies using small samples. The data are remarkably consistent in showing that kids of gay-lesbian-bisexual parents are no different than kids of heterosexual couples with regard to mental health, etc.

Geography Plays a Part in Acceptance

People around here might say that all these worries about whether gays and lesbians can be good parents, and will the kids be OK—that it sounds very old hat, that we've long since moved on. So I'm wondering what the research shows about the importance of where you live. Does geography matter?

Oh, absolutely, where you live makes a huge difference. I looked at people from all over—Nebraska, Texas, Utah. A couple in rural Pennsylvania, for instance—two gay men with a black son—who are so much more aware of their visibility as a family. Some of them wind up moving to areas that are more progressive or they end up spending all of their money to send their child to private school. People in progressive areas always say, "We really haven't had any discrimination because of where we live." But then they say that when they go to other places, they still get the stares, the weird questions, the comments.

How did you get interested in this subject?

Ever since high school, I'd wanted to be a psychologist and later on, I got interested in diversity. There are hundreds of studies about the transition to parenthood that heterosexual couples make. But there were none about the parenting challenges facing same-sex couples. In graduate school, I started looking at that.

How did you do that?

I found 35 lesbian couples around the country and followed them from before they became parents to afterwards. I did prenatal interviews, with each partner separately. They also filled out 30-page questionnaires, about their families, friends, their expectations and hopes, how they thought they'd divide the work of parenting. Then I interviewed them again three months after the baby was born, and again three years later.

Same-Sex Parents Identify Themselves First as Parents

What were some of your findings?

In the first months, the nonbiological moms had to figure out their role. They weren't the birth mom, they weren't breastfeeding, and they're not the father. They had to invent and explain their role to their families and to the outside world, that they're not less of a parent, or less involved.

How had becoming parents changed their identities?

By and large it was that "We're parents now," and that other stuff about being gay is not as relevant.

Probably the most interesting was a distinction between the biological and nonbiological moms. The biological moms who were breastfeeding spent more time with the baby—and the nonbiological mother often had to go back to work quickly because she couldn't get maternity or paternity leave. They all had high expectations for equality from the start, but the demands of breastfeeding made a difference and that was something a few of them were struggling with at three months.

The Census Includes Unwed and Gay Partners

Not every gay couple that is married, or aspiring to marry, has children, but an increasing number do: [As of 2009,] approximately 1 in 5 male same-sex couples and 1 in 3 female same-sex couples are raising children, up from 1 in 20 male couples and 1 in 5 female couples in 1990.

Lisa Belkin, "What's Good for the Kids,"
New York Times, *November 5, 2009.*

Same-Sex Parents Encourage Their Children to Be Tolerant and Independent

What about later on?

There's much less distinction in their roles, the division of labor is more balanced. Same-sex couples are more likely to have more fluid arrangements in terms of work. One will work part-time and one full-time and then they'll switch off. They're more adaptive. At three years, a minority of them felt the birth mother was still the primary mother, and that the child still preferred her. In a very few couples, it was something they were unhappy with, but they didn't know how to undo it.

You mentioned that same-sex parents are more likely to foster independence rather than conformity in their children. Why is that?

I think it's because of the challenges they faced in their own lives. They're much more likely to be tolerant, to encourage, for example, their children to play with a wider range of toys—to encourage a girl to play with both dolls and trucks. Girls (of lesbian parents) are more likely to have higher career aspirations.

What about that hot-button question, are the children of gay parents more likely to be gay?

They're just not as gender stereotyped. They're more open, less constrained. The girls are more likely to be open to same-sex relationships, to say, "I can imagine it." But that doesn't mean it will translate into future behavior. It means they're saying, "I don't think it's unusual, I don't think it's gross."

Does any of the research show the opposite—that some kids of same-sex parents want to be anything but gay, not because they don't love their parents, but because they've been dealing with "difference" all their lives?

That is exactly what I found. These kids are tired of defending their families and they're very aware that their parents feel this pressure to produce straight kids. They're so aware, growing up in the lens of media scrutiny, they feel they need to say, if I feel like screaming at my mom, it has nothing to do with the fact that she's gay!

Boys Might Be Teased More than Girls

What does the research say about the differences between boys and girls raised by two moms. Are the experiences different?

They don't appear to be all that different. Boys may be more likely than girls to be teased for having two moms, which may have to do with other kids' issues of masculinity and homophobia.

When I asked couples before they had children whether they had a preference for a boy or girl, I found that some gay men were more anxious about having a boy because of worries that a son will be teased more. Or they'd say, we're not really sports people, what if we can't do that part of parenting? They'd say a girl would just be easier. Lesbian couples don't have that same anxiety.

Does that suggest that dealing with the outside world is harder for two dads than it is for two moms?

I think so. When people see a man or two men parenting their kids at the park, they tend to assume that they can't possibly know what they're doing, that they can't be naturally nurturing and caretaking. I can't tell you how many men told me they're asked in those situations, do you need help, are you giving Mom the day off?

> "Men and women bring diversity to parenting; each makes unique contributions to the rearing of children that can't be replicated by the other. Mothers and fathers simply are not interchangeable."

A Family Must Include a Mother and a Father

Trayce Hansen

In the following viewpoint, Trayce Hansen argues that the benefits provided by having a man and a woman as parents far outweigh the love that same-sex parents offer their children. She contends that heterosexual parents offer their children a balance and stability that same-sex couples cannot. She further maintains that gay and lesbian couples cannot provide the appropriate role models that children need. Hansen is a psychologist who has written extensively about marriage, parenting, homosexuality, and differences between men and women.

As you read, consider the following questions:

1. According to Hansen, from which parent does a child receive "unconditional-leaning love"?

Trayce Hansen, "Love Isn't Enough: 5 Reasons Why Same-Sex Marriage Will Harm Children," www.drtraycehansen.com, October 16, 2007. Reproduced by permission of the author.

2. In the author's view, what does having a relationship with a parent of the opposite sex do for a child?

3. According to the author, what is the "implicit and explicit message" that children learn from same-sex marriage?

Proponents of same-sex marriage believe the only thing children really need is love. Based on that supposition, they conclude it's just as good for children to be raised by loving parents of the same sex as it is to be raised by loving parents of the opposite sex. Unfortunately, that basic assumption—and all that flows from it—is false. Because love *isn't* enough!

All else being equal, children do best when raised by a married mother and father. It's within this environment that children are most likely to be exposed to the emotional and psychological experiences they need in order to thrive.

Men and women bring diversity to parenting; each makes unique contributions to the rearing of children that can't be replicated by the other. Mothers and fathers simply are not interchangeable. Two women can both be good mothers, but neither can be a good father.

So here are five reasons why it's in the best interest of children to be raised by both a mother and a father.

Mothers and Fathers Are Not Interchangeable

First, mother-love and father-love—though equally important—are qualitatively different and produce distinct parent-child attachments. Specifically, it's the combination of the unconditional-leaning love of a mother and the conditional-leaning love of a father that's essential to a child's development. Either of these forms of love without the other can be problematic because what a child needs is the complementary balance the two types of parental love and attachment provide.

Only heterosexual parents offer children the opportunity to develop relationships with a parent of the same as well as the opposite sex. Relationships with both sexes early in life make it easier for a child to relate to both sexes later in life. For a girl, that means she'll better understand and appropriately interact with the world of men and be more comfortable in the world of women. And for a boy, the converse will hold true. Having a relationship with "the other"—an opposite-sexed parent—also increases the likelihood that a child will be more empathetic and less narcissistic.

Children Learn Appropriate Behavior from the Parent of the Same Gender

Secondly, children progress through predictable and necessary developmental stages. Some stages require more from a mother, while others require more from a father. For example, during infancy, babies of both sexes tend to do better in the care of their mother. Mothers are more attuned to the subtle needs of their infants and thus are more appropriately responsive. However, at some point, if a young boy is to become a competent man, he must detach from his mother and instead identify with his father. A fatherless boy doesn't have a man with whom to identify and is more likely to have trouble forming a healthy masculine identity.

A father teaches a boy how to properly channel his aggressive and sexual drives. A mother can't show a son how to control his impulses because she's not a man and doesn't have the same urges as one. A father also commands a form of respect from a boy that a mother doesn't—a respect more likely to keep the boy in line. And those are the two primary reasons why boys without fathers are more likely to become delinquent and end up incarcerated.

Father-need is also built into the psyche of girls. There are times in a girl's life when only a father will do. For instance, a father offers a daughter a safe, nonsexual place to experience her first male-female relationship and have her femininity affirmed. When a girl doesn't have a father to fill that role, she's more likely to become promiscuous in a misguided attempt to satisfy her inborn hunger for male attention and validation.

Overall, fathers play a restraining role in the lives of their children. They restrain sons from acting out antisocially, and daughters from acting out sexually. When there's no father to perform this function, dire consequences often result both for the fatherless children and for the society in which these children act out their losses.

Third, boys and girls need an opposite-sexed parent to help them moderate their own gender-linked inclinations. As example, boys generally embrace reason over emotion, rules over relationships, risk-taking over caution, and standards over compassion, while girls generally embrace the reverse. An opposite-sexed parent helps a child keep his or her own natural proclivities in check by teaching—verbally and nonverbally—the worth of the opposing tendencies. That teaching not only facilitates moderation, but it also expands the child's world—helping the child see beyond his or her own limited vantage point.

Same-Sex Parenting Leads to Unsafe Sex and Sexual Confusion

Fourth, same-sex marriage will increase sexual confusion and sexual experimentation by young people. The implicit and explicit message of same-sex marriage is that *all* choices are equally acceptable and desirable. So, even children from traditional homes—influenced by the all-sexual-options-are-equal message—will grow up thinking it doesn't matter whom one relates to sexually or marries. Holding such a belief will lead some—if not many—impressionable young people to consider sexual and marital arrangements they never would have contemplated previously. And children from homosexual families, who are already more likely to experiment sexually, would do so to an even greater extent, because not only was nontraditional sexuality role-modeled by their parents, it was also approved by their society.

There is no question that human sexuality is *pliant* [flexible]. Think of ancient Greece or Rome—among many other early civilizations—where male homosexuality and bisexuality were nearly ubiquitous. This was not so because most of those men were born with a "gay gene," rather it was because homosexuality was condoned by those societies. That which a society sanctions, it gets more of.

And fifth, if society permits same-sex marriage, it also will have to allow other types of marriage. The legal logic is simple: If prohibiting same-sex marriage is discriminatory, then disallowing polygamous marriage, polyamorous marriage [both of which include more than two individuals], or any other marital grouping will also be deemed discriminatory. The emotional and psychological ramifications of these assorted arrangements on the developing psyches and sexuality of children would be disastrous. And what happens to the children of these alternative marriages if the union dissolves and each parent then "remarries"? Those children could end up with four fathers, or two fathers and four mothers, or, you fill in the blank.

Certainly homosexual couples can be just as loving as heterosexual couples, but children require *more* than love. They need the distinctive qualities and the complementary natures of a male and female parent.

The accumulated wisdom of over 5,000 years has concluded that the ideal marital and parental configuration is composed of one man and one woman. Arrogantly disregarding such time-tested wisdom, and using children as guinea pigs in a radical experiment, is risky at best, and cataclysmic at worst.

Same-sex marriage definitely isn't in the best interest of children. And although we empathize with those homosexuals who long to be married and parent children, we mustn't allow our compassion for them to trump our compassion for children. In a contest between the desires of some homosexuals and the needs of *all* children, we can't allow the children to lose.

"*The argument that is most commonly used to denounce gay parenting is not the threat of promiscuity or pedophilia. It is simply the old fallback: the importance of two opposite-sex parents.*"

A Family Does Not Have to Include a Mother and a Father

Ellen Friedrichs

In the following viewpoint, Ellen Friedrichs contends that gays and lesbians often outshine heterosexuals in raising children. She argues that children with same-sex parents are more likely to do well in school and have fewer social problems. Friedrichs maintains that gays and lesbians take the idea of parenting more seriously because it is more difficult for them to become parents. Friedrichs is a sex educator who teaches high school and college classes in New York City.

As you read, consider the following questions:

1. According to Friedrichs, why does Kellen Kaiser think that gay "parenting is less done on automatic"?

2. According to the author, how did Charles Cooper justify his support of California's Proposition 8?

Ellen Friedrichs, "Hey Conservatives—Gays Are Better Parents than You," AlterNet.org, July 16, 2010. Reproduced by permission.

3. In the opinion of Shanie Israel and Mary Valentine, what will "being part of the queer community" give their daughter?

When I ask 29-year-old Kellen Kaiser if I can get her take on a few new studies demonstrating the benefits to gay parenting, she jokingly warns me that she's biased.

That isn't really surprising given the family that the L.A.-based actress and writer grew up in. Born after three lesbian friends decided to co-parent (and one ultimately became pregnant), Kaiser was also raised by her biological mother's long-term partner, alongside a brother who was the product of a known gay sperm donor.

Though this model of parenting may be unfamiliar to the average American, (and the specifics of this particular family are, of course, not characteristic of the entire LGBT [lesbian, gay, bisexual, and transgender] community), to Kaiser, the strengths are obvious. As she says, "I certainly feel like I gained from being exposed to so many different and wonderful adults in my life. I think gay parents are more intentional on the whole than the average straight parent. Parenting is less done on automatic. Gay families tend to reexamine and reform traditions to the particular needs of their families and children."

She's not alone in this assessment, and research is beginning to back her up.

Robert-Jay Green, the executive director of the Rockway Institute for LGBT psychology and public policy has looked at the experiences of gay men who became fathers using gestational or "surrogate" mothers. In April [2010], in a paper published in the *Journal of GLBT Family Studies*, he and his colleagues reported that gay dads were more likely than straight [dads] to put their children before their careers, make significant changes in their lives to accommodate a child, and to strengthen bonds with extended families after becoming parents. He tells me, "The conservative argument is that children raised by gay parents will suffer by virtue of the fact of the parents' sexual orientation. But there is lots of anecdotal evidence that children raised by gay parents are doing just fine and the central orientation of the parents, in and of itself, has no negative impact on the children." His upcoming work will focus on translating such anecdotes into research as he studies the psychological outcomes of children raised by heterosexual parents compared to children conceived through surrogacy and raised by gay male parents.

Though Green will be the first to look at this particular population, in June [2010], the results of an almost two-decade-long study of the children of lesbian moms came out in the journal *Pediatrics*. This reported that not only do such children do as well as the children of straight married parents, but in some key ways, they do even better. Indeed, after following the children of lesbian moms for their first 17 years, researchers Nanette Gartrell and Henny Bos determined that compared to other teens, these kids were more likely to succeed academically, and were less likely to have social problems, break rules or exhibit aggressive behavior.

And in a recent review article published [in January 2010] in the *Journal of Marriage and Family*, sociologists Judith Stacey and Timothy Biblarz looked at the results of 81 studies of gay-, lesbian- and heterosexual-headed families. They found that benefits usually associated with families made up of a mother and a father are just as apparent in families with two women parents. And while the pair acknowledged that there simply wasn't enough research on gay male parents to definitively make the same claim, they emphasized that all evidence indicated that the results would be similar.

Studies Refute Antigay Stereotypes

Such reports, not to mention positive reflections by the children of gay parents, are probably pretty mind-boggling to the type of person who is convinced that gay men are pedophiles, lesbians bitter man-haters, and that both will raise children who are not only scarred by endless school-yard taunts, but who are also likely to grow up to be homosexuals themselves. (Note to those folks: both Kaiser and her brother identify as straight).

Yet arguments against gay parenting persist. For example, the extremist organization Family Research Council (which was founded by the now shamed George Rekers [a conservative leader who is accused of being secretly gay]) claims on [its] website that, "The raising of children is inimical [hostile] to the typical homosexual lifestyle, which as we have seen typically involves a revolving bedroom door. With the added problem of high rates of intimate partner violence, such households constitute a dangerous and unstable environment for children. Homosexuals and lesbians are unsuitable role models for children because of their lifestyle."

Such unfounded assertions have been repeated enough that even without any real proof, they are regularly used to justify things like rejecting adoption petitions by gay men and lesbians (there is an outright ban in Florida [that was overturned on September 22, 2010]), or denying a nonbiological gay parent rights during a custody dispute.

Still, the argument that is most commonly used to denounce gay parenting is not the threat of promiscuity or pedophilia. It is simply the old fallback: the importance of two opposite-sex parents. This was invoked in June during the hearings over California's Prop 8 (which stripped gays and lesbians of their brief ability to legally marry in that state) when Charles Cooper, the lawyer representing the sponsors of the 2008 ballot measure, justified his position by citing the "commonsense belief that children do best when they are raised by their own mother and father."

But do they really? Nope. Even this "commonsense belief" is really just that. A belief. Not a fact.

Families Do Not Need a Mother and a Father to Be Complete

Children raised by homosexuals know there is nothing wrong with their families and learn at a young age to accept people for who they are, no matter how different they may look or act. Children who are raised in homosexual families still receive the same love and care as other children and grow up to be just as happy and healthy, while also having the added benefit of growing up more open-minded than most of their peers.

Tammye Nash, "Gay and Lesbian Parents: Teaching Kids It's OK to Be Different," Dallasvoice.com, April 6, 2010.

Gays and Lesbians Take Parenting More Seriously

Stacey and Biblarz explain in their review article that research to date has not demonstrated that a married mother and father automatically create the best environment for children. As they write, "In fact, based strictly on the published science, one could argue that two women parent better on average than a woman and a man, or at least than a woman and man with a traditional division of family labor. Lesbian co-parents seem to outperform comparable married heterosexual, biological parents on several measures, even while being denied the substantial privileges of marriage."

There are plenty of reasons behind this, of course. As many have observed, gay men and lesbians typically do not become parents accidentally. Most have made conscious and complicated decisions in order to parent. And while having children intentionally doesn't automatically mean one will do a better job at it (Jon and Kate Gosselin come to mind [a divorced celebrity couple with eight children]), it sure gives these parents a leg up.

Additionally, multiple studies have demonstrated that the children of gay parents tend to be raised in financially stable households with fewer rigid gender divisions, by parents who are typically more involved with their children. These parents, studies have found, are also more likely to discuss issues like sexuality and discrimination, have support systems in place and enjoy a more egalitarian relationship with each other. All of these issues appear to create healthier long-term outcomes for kids.

The Gay and Lesbian Community Offers a Strong Support Network

This seems reflected in the parenting goal of Shanie Israel and Mary Valentine, a Brooklyn, N.Y., lesbian couple and parents to 20-month-old, Avner, who list giving their daughter a sense of community, social justice and pride in being a woman as priorities. They also feel that being a part of the queer community will give their daughter a lifetime support network, something that many people worry we are losing in a world where more people than ever report feeling socially isolated. As Israel says, "I think Avner will grow up in a much more open household than I did. Less secrets, more honest and open questions and answers. That can't hurt a kid." Ultimately, regardless of their views on gay parenting, that's a view many people probably share.

Obviously, every family will be different and it is impossible [to] make direct comparisons between all gay and all straight parents. But in some key ways there are important advantages to gay parenting that may come from holding certain values, living outside the majority and having to make very deliberate parenting choices. Gay families are both more visible and more accepted than ever before—certainly a positive trend—but also one that might affect parenting style. Kellen Kaiser speculates that with growing acceptance might come a different kind of leveling of the playing field. "Maybe radicals make better parents is the truth. Gay parents are becoming more mainstream and maybe in the long run they won't be that much better, and it will all average out." Like so many other things in life, this too, remains to be seen.

> "The desperate determination to honor
> gay rights undermines such fundamen-
> tal values as the importance of mother-
> hood and the state's obligation to con-
> sider the welfare of the child."

Custody Case
Highlights Artificiality
of Same Sex Marriage

Michael Medved

In this viewpoint, Michael Medved maintains that the custody issues created when same-sex couples break up are more complicated than those that occur when a man and woman end a marriage. He contends that same-sex relationships show complete disregard for the idea of family because only one of the same-sex parents will have a biological connection to the child involved. Medved, a nationally syndicated radio talk show host, is the author of such books as Hollywood vs. America *and* Right Turns.

As you read, consider the following questions:

1. According to the viewpoint, why did the relationship between Lisa Miller and Janet Jenkins end?

2. In the author's view, child custody is always granted to mothers except in cases of what?

3. According to Medved, on what does Janet Jenkins's parental standing rest?

A nasty custody case in Virginia highlights the way that the relentless push for same-sex marriage threatens our core understanding of the nature of family. The desperate determination to honor gay rights undermines such fundamental values as the importance of motherhood and the state's obligation to consider the welfare of the child.

The basic facts of the current dispute remain uncontested. In the late 1990s, Lisa Miller and Janet Jenkins began a lesbian relationship, and they secured a civil union in the state of Vermont in 2000. Shortly thereafter, Miller became pregnant through artificial insemination from a sperm donor, with the understanding that she and Jenkins would raise the resulting child as a couple. After the baby's first birthday, however, Miller renounced homosexuality, became an Evangelical Christian and decided to raise her child, Isabella, on her own. The two women sought legal dissolution of their relationship in the Vermont Family Court and the judge, William D. Cohen, awarded custody to the birth mother but provided extensive visitation rights for the mother's rejected girlfriend. For several years, Miller resisted sharing her daughter with Jenkins, employing various legal strategies to challenge the court order. At one point, the Supreme Court of the United States declined to hear the case.

Finally, on November 20, 2009, Judge Cohen found Miller in contempt of court for continuing to deny access to her daughter, now seven years old. He also changed his decision regarding custody, now awarding custody to Jenkins, who bore no biological connection to the child and played no significant role in her upbringing after the baby's first year. Courts in both Virginia and Vermont backed Jenkins's claims on the baby—claims that received potent free legal backing from both the ACLU and the gay-rights-oriented Lambda Legal. The governmental authorities ordered Lisa Miller to hand over little Isabella to Janet Jenkins, a woman the child hardly knew, on January 1st, at 1 PM, at the home of Ms. Jenkins's parents in Falls Church, Virginia. Ms. Miller failed to appear as directed, and is presumed to have become a fugitive with her daughter.

Regardless of the final outcome of this sad story, the case demonstrates the way that the militant gay rights agenda trumps long-standing patterns and preferences in family law.

First, and most obviously, family courts have always tilted toward the mother in custody disputes as many brokenhearted ex-husbands have discovered to their pain and regret. Judges and child welfare agencies give the mother principal custody except in cases of blatant abuse, neglect or irresponsibility. No one accuses Lisa Miller of such mistreatment, and yet she is stripped of responsibility for her seven-year-old daughter by an ex-lover with no biological connection to the child—a woman who is surely less deserving of parental rights than a birth father would have been. Activists in the father's rights movement can testify to the one-sided dismissal of their claims, and wonder at the far more favorable treatment in this case for a non-related female lover.

This raises another startling aspect of the government's role in this conflict: the rejection of biological connection as an overriding and significant factor. In many well-publicized cases, courts have awarded special consideration to birth mothers (and even birth fathers) in cases of surrogacy and adoption, even allowing these genetic connections to shatter loving homes and invalidate explicit contracts. Americans will also remember the wrenching case of Elián González, who was taken from a nurturing household of his relatives in Florida and brought back to Cuba at the demand of a biological fa-ther he hadn't seen in years. It's hard to think of a non-related, heterosexual adoptive parent in a high-profile battle who has been awarded custody precedence over a birth parent the way the courts have given precedence to this non-related homosexual partner.

Finally, the judges in both Vermont and Virginia relied upon legalisms and selective precedent and paid scant attention to the welfare of the child. Yes, Lisa Miller harmed her own standing when she defied court orders to provide access to her daughter, and she perhaps fatally undermined her case in her initial request for dissolution of her civil union when she requested child support from her former partner. As the argument developed, however, she more and more clearly wanted only to raise her child free of interference from an old lover with whom she shared no further relationship.

Aside from the relevant legal arguments, there's an inescapable underlying question concerning the whole dispute: In what sense would a seven-year-old girl benefit from regular parental contact with an unrelated female now bitterly estranged from her mother? It's easy to understand why Janet Jenkins might desire a parental role with the girl she remembered as an infant, but how would this intrusion into a growing child's life help the youngster's sense of stability or security? Given Lisa Miller's decisive rejection of homosexuality, should the government insist that a seven-year-old must be fully apprised of her mother's lesbian past? Is the societal goal of instilling tolerance and acceptance in a little girl more important than a mother's right to raise a daughter according to her own lights?

With Ms. Miller and little Isabella living, at least for the time being, as apparent fugitives from the court system, it's easy to feel sorry for the girl, who's been victimized by her mother's bad decisions, the stubborn selfishness of her mother's former lover, and the shortsighted officiousness of the courts. But even if the authorities apprehend the runaway mother-daughter pair, it would hardly constitute a joyous development for the seven-year-old to be taken away from the only mom she can remember and placed under the control of an implacable stranger (and her gay advocate lawyers).

The worst part of the case is the creation of a new position of entitlement awarded to Janet Jenkins on the basis of gay sex alone. If she'd been a non-romantic roommate of the little girl's mother, or even a dear old auntie who helped with the infant's care, it's hard to imagine the courts would have granted her custody years later. But the illogical insistence that gay partnerships must be treated as identical to procreative heterosexual unions gave Jenkins special claims to parenthood based more on the nature of her relationship to the mother than to the history of her connection to the child. In any event, the synthetic, unnatural nature of those claims based almost entirely on the securing of civil union status from the Vermont bureaucracy some nine years ago means that Jenkins's parental standing rests on an artificial governmental construct, on forms and signatures, rather than on any sort of organic or experiential connection.

One of the most common arguments by gay-marriage advocates involves the insistence that the expansion of matrimonial rights will merely enlarge marital opportunities, with no impact at all on existing couples or the institution itself. The Miller-Jenkins case shows the absurdity of this contention and demonstrates the way that redefining marriage inevitably changes parenthood as well, turning the most fundamental, natural, elemental human relationship of mother and child into an officially sanctioned fiction altogether dependent on governmental fiat.

> *"Children of gay or lesbian parents whose families break down face unique challenges as a result of a patchwork of varying antigay laws from state to state."*

The Legal System Is Unfair to Gay Parents

Camilla Taylor

In the following viewpoint, Camilla Taylor argues that difficult custody cases become much more complicated because of state antigay laws as well as the often irresponsible behavior of the parents involved in the cases. She asserts that state laws are biased against same-sex couples. Taylor is the marriage project director of the Midwest regional office of Lambda Legal, which is a national organization dedicated to achieving and protecting the civil rights of lesbians, gay men, bisexuals, transgender people, and individuals with HIV.

As you read, consider the following questions:

1. According to Taylor, how do some gay or lesbian parents sacrifice legal protections for children of other gay and lesbian parents during a custody battle?

Camilla Taylor, "Gay v. Gay Custody Battles," *Of Counsel*, vol. 5, no. 4, September 2009. Reproduced by permission.

2. According to the author, on what basis did Lambda Legal argue that the Oklahoma "Adoption Invalidation Law" was unconstitutional?

3. According to Taylor, how did *Giancaspro v. Congleton* leave the involved children in "legal limbo"?

Child custody cases are among the most tragic on our docket. Each involves a child or children whose world has turned upside down while parents battle with each other over issues such as child support or visitation. Regardless of whether a case involves gay or nongay parents, children often suffer terribly when parents go to court because they cannot agree on how to resolve their dispute over child custody.

Many State Laws Are Unfair to Gays and Lesbians

However, children of gay or lesbian parents whose families break down face unique challenges as a result of a patchwork of varying antigay laws from state to state. Additionally, courts in some states are unwilling to recognize that a child may have two parents of the same sex, or may be hesitant to award custody or visitation to a person who has reared a child from birth as his or her parent, but who has neither a biological nor adoptive relationship to the child. The children in these families are exceptionally vulnerable. In the past year and a half [since early 2007], Lambda Legal lawyers have appeared in cases to protect a child's relationship to a lesbian or gay parent in numerous states including Alabama, Georgia, Missouri, Florida, Arizona, Ohio, Michigan, Virginia, North Carolina, New York, Louisiana and West Virginia.

What makes many of these cases particularly heartbreaking is that some gay or lesbian parents are willing to make use of antigay laws in order to gain advantage in a bitter personal dispute with their former partners—even at the expense of their own children's welfare. In numerous cases, we battle arguments raised by certain gay or lesbian individuals that a court should deny any recognition or protection to his or her former partner's relationship with their child based solely on the family's nontraditional structure—that the parents are of the same sex, are unmarried or that the child has no genetic link to his or her second parent—and without any regard to the child's best interests. In such cases, certain gay or lesbian parents ask courts to throw out what is often settled law protecting a child's bonded relationship to the adult or adults who have parented the child from birth. Too often, these parents also argue that courts should rely on recently passed measures banning same-sex couples from marriage to sever their child's relationship with a former partner. These individuals abandon their parental responsibility of putting their children's needs before their own selfish desires to punish a former partner at any cost, and in the process are willing to sacrifice vital legal protections for untold numbers of other children with gay or lesbian and/or unmarried parents.

Antigay Laws Are Used Often Against an Ex-Partner

In one recent example, Lambda Legal appeared in an Ohio trial court this summer [2009] to oppose a motion filed by a biological mother who sought to undo the adoption order that she had jointly sought and obtained in California years earlier with her former partner. The adoption decree designated both partners as legal parents to the child whose conception via anonymous donor insemination they had planned together—and whom they had reared together from birth. After the couple moved to Ohio, their relationship broke down and they jointly filed a complaint asking an Ohio court to allocate custody in their child's best interests. Months later, the biological mother found new counsel and changed course. She filed a motion demanding that the court dismiss her complaint and sever the child's relationship to her former partner, claiming that Ohio courts need not accord full faith and credit to California adoption decrees involving same-sex parents. Her claim was based on the theory that such adoptions would not be permissible under Ohio law and that adoptions by same-sex couples conflict with Ohio's antigay constitutional amendment concerning marriage. Her motion made no reference to her child's best interests nor to the potentially devastating consequences of eliminating a parent from a child's life. Lambda Legal appeared on behalf of the nonbiological mother to lay out settled Ohio and federal law requiring respect for adoption decrees entered in other states. We also pointed out that Ohio's constitutional amendment barring marriage for same-sex couples, while spiteful and discriminatory, is legally irrelevant in parenting disputes. In Ohio, as elsewhere, child custody determinations concern children's relationships to the adults who care for them and not the adults' relationships to each other. Further, Ohio courts may not discriminate based on sex, marital status or sexual orientation in adjudicating child custody. We await a decision from the trial court in this case.

Our optimism that we will achieve a positive result in this case for the child and her nonbiological mother derives in part from our work in other states firmly establishing that courts of one state must respect and accord full faith and credit to adoption decrees entered in another state. In *Finstuen v. Edmondson*, Lambda Legal won a major victory before the 10th Circuit Court of Appeals in a case that struck down an Oklahoma law so extreme that it threatened to make children adopted by same-sex couples in other states legal orphans when the families are in Oklahoma. The "Adoption Invalidation Law," hastily passed at the end of the 2004 Oklahoma legislative session, stated that Oklahoma "shall not recognize an adoption by more than one individual of the same sex from any other state or foreign jurisdiction." Lambda Legal argued that the law was unconstitutional based on the

U.S. Constitution's guarantees of equal protection and due process, as well as the full faith and credit clause. The Court of Appeals held that the statute indeed violates the Constitution by refusing to honor adoption decrees obtained in other states. The ruling is important not only in Oklahoma, but also to families across the United States—and we cited it in the Ohio brief we filed this summer.

In the next month [October 2009], Lambda Legal will appear before the 5th Circuit Court of Appeals to defend another recent victory affirming the principle that adoption decrees in one state must be recognized in courts of another state. In *Adar v. Smith*, Lambda Legal represents Oren Adar and Mickey Smith, a gay couple who adopted their Louisiana-born son in 2006 in a New York court, where a judge issued an adoption decree. When Smith attempted [to] get a new birth certificate for their child, in part so he could add his son to his health insurance, the Louisiana registrar told him that Louisiana does not recognize adoption by unmarried parents and so could not issue it. Lambda Legal won a victory before the U.S. District Court, which ordered the Louisiana state registrar [Darlene Smith] to honor the New York adoption of a baby boy by a same-sex couple, saying her continued failure to do so violated the U.S. Constitution. "This sends a strong message to state officials across the country that the Constitution requires them to respect the parent-child relationships established by adoption decrees regardless of the state where the decree is entered," said Ken Upton, [Lambda Legal] senior staff attorney, after the ruling. "State officials may not punish children by denying them a birth certificate simply because they disapprove of their parents."

Using the Law to Help Nonbiological Parents

As a recent Michigan custody case demonstrates, these full faith and credit precedents create significant protection for

Working Cooperatively in Same-Sex Divorce

The federal ban against same-sex marriages not only throws up roadblocks for LGBT [lesbian, gay, bisexual, and transgender] couples wishing to wed. It also complicates their divorce proceedings when the relationship sours. . . .

"Given that DOMA [the Defense of Marriage Act] denies same-gender couples the options straight people have to organize our finances when divorcing, it provides even more incentive for same-gender couples to work cooperatively in our divorces," [says] attorney Charlie Spiegel.

Matthew S. Bajko,
"DOMA Complicates Gay Divorces,"
Bay Area Reporter, February 16, 2012.

nonbiological parents battling the argument raised by a former partner that their adoption decree is worthless because it was entered in another state. In *Giancaspro v. Congleton*, Lambda Legal and the American Civil Liberties Union [ACLU] of Michigan represented Diane Giancaspro, a lesbian mother, who filed papers in August 2007 asking a Michigan trial court to determine custody of the three children she and her ex-partner, Lisa Ann Congleton, adopted together in Illinois before moving as a family to Michigan. When the couple's relationship ended, Congleton moved to dismiss Giancaspro's custody complaint, arguing that their adoption was invalid under the Michigan Child Custody Act and citing Michigan's antigay constitutional amendment regarding marriage. The trial court granted Congleton's motion, holding both parties' parental rights unenforceable in Michigan. The ruling called into question whether the children were effectively orphans in Michigan and whether both parents would be able to do such essential things as authorize medical treatment at a public hospital, enroll them in school or recover their lost child from a local police department. The trial court's ruling left the children in legal limbo, without an enforceable legal connection to either parent. Lambda Legal and the ACLU of Michigan appealed on behalf of Diane Giancaspro. In February 2009, the Michigan Court of Appeals reversed the trial court, relying upon *Finstuen* and other full faith and credit precedents, and held that courts cannot refuse to hear a child custody case simply because the case involves children whose parents are lesbians, ruling that there is no gay exception to Michigan's child custody laws.

Case by case, we are creating positive law that protects children by affirming that adoption decrees must be recognized across state lines. As the web of precedent expands, it becomes easier in each case to stamp out attempts to sever a child's adoptive relationship to his or her legal parent. However, it remains a tragedy that we have to assert these arguments at all, particularly in cases pitting one gay parent against another. As a community, we must do more to reinforce how damaging a parent's efforts to void his or her own child's adoption decree can be—both to children and to all of us. These arguments are not only a betrayal of our children's trust, but also of the hard-fought advances that we have made in recent years establishing respect in the courts for the civil rights of LGBT [lesbian, gay, bisexual, and transgender] parents.

| *"More parents and more children are finding that traditional notions of the nuclear family don't accurately reflect their lives and relationships."*

The Definition of Parenthood Must Be Revised

Drake Bennett

In the following viewpoint, Drake Bennett considers whether the definitions of family and parenthood need to be redefined as emerging assisted reproductive technologies enable gays and lesbians to have children. Advocates of rethinking how many parents a child can have maintain that society must change to reflect children's lives, according to Bennett. Opponents contend that such changes will result in more complicated custody cases and will make life more difficult for the children involved. Bennett is a staff writer for the Boston Globe.

As you read, consider the following questions:

1. According to Bennett, what kind of law set two as the maximum number of parents a child can have?

2. According to the author, in which states have the most third-party adoptions taken place?

3. In Bennett's view, what was the most important change in parent law during the twentieth century?

"To an unconventional family." That's what Paul, the roguish restaurateur and sperm donor, raises his glass to in this summer's [2010's] movie *The Kids Are All Right*. Paul is, he has recently discovered, the biological father of two teenage children, one by each partner in a long-term lesbian couple. Contacted by the kids, he has come into their lives and has begun to compete for the affections of various members of the family he unknowingly helped create. Complications—funny, then sad—ensue.

The film's family is indeed unconventional, but it is not unique. In the age of assisted reproductive technology, the increasing acceptance of same-sex partnerships, and a steady growth in "blended" families, more parents and more children are finding that traditional notions of the nuclear family don't accurately reflect their lives and relationships.

A Two-Parent Family Is No Longer the Norm

Still, even in a time of changing attitudes about who can be a parent, the legal and social definition of a family still has certain rules—a family can be run by a single mom or a single dad and, increasingly, by two moms or two dads, but it can't have three parents, or four. For a long, long time—going back to when the English common law first started codifying such things—the law has set the maximum number of parents a child can have as two. Only two people, in other words, can enjoy the unique set of rights to determine a child's life—and the unique set of responsibilities for the child's welfare—that legal parenthood entails. That matches how most people think about parenthood: Two people, after all, are how many it usually takes to make a baby in the first place.

Now a few family-law scholars have begun to argue that there is nothing special about the number two—if three or four or five adults have a parental relationship with a child, the law should recognize them all as parents. . . .

Redefining Parenthood Will Lead to Emotional and Legal Problems

In a few recent cases, courts seem to have agreed with the calls for multiple parents. But critics argue that tinkering with the definition of parenthood in this way threatens to dilute the sense of obligation that being a parent has always carried, and that increasing the number of legal parents only raises the likelihood that family disputes will arise and get messy and find their way into court. Not to mention that having judges routinely declare that Heather has two mommies and three daddies would represent a radical cultural shift, and one that, like gay marriage, many will find threatening.

Ultimately, the legal definition of parenthood is part of a broader philosophical question: What is a family? And what is it for? While some scholars have focused on expanding the number of parents, others argue that the law needs to do more to recognize the social context in which families exist, and the extent to which child care is actually performed by people who aren't part of the nuclear family at all.

And as supporters of revising the definition of parenthood point out, there's nothing tidy or biologically preordained about today's prevailing notion of parentage, one that often has to shoehorn families jumbled and reassembled by divorce, adoption, and reproductive technology into one standard model, in ways that can prove disruptive to the families in question.

"The law determines what makes someone a legal parent, not marriage, not biology. Those things don't determine who is a parent, the law does," says [family-law professor Nancy] Polikoff.

When Sharon Tanenbaum and Matty Person, a married lesbian couple in San Francisco, decided to have a child together, it wasn't hard to figure out who they wanted the sperm donor to be. Bill Hirsh was one of Sharon's oldest friends; they had known each other, Sharon says, "since we were born, more or less." Their fathers had been best friends in college, and Sharon and Bill had grown up spending summers together and calling each other's parents aunts and uncles.

Sharon, Matty, and Bill agreed that Bill would be more than just a source of genetic material—they wanted him to be a father. When Sharon had a son, Jesse, in 1994, the boy lived with Sharon and Matty, but growing up he spent one day a week with Bill and Bill's same-sex partner, Thompson. In addition, the whole family would gather once a week for dinner.

Legally, however, Sharon and Bill were Jesse's parents, and that put Matty in a potentially precarious position. "Let's say I died in some terrible car crash or whatever and Matty had no legal rights, and let's say she and Billy had a falling-out or one of my parents or brother wanted to take care of Jesse," Sharon says. In that case, Matty could have had Jesse taken away from her altogether.

At the same time, no one in the family wanted to force Bill to give up his parental status. So, when Jesse was 4, their lawyer persuaded the San Francisco Superior Court to allow Matty to do a third-parent adoption. The move, which had little precedent, gave Jesse three parents, three people who, in the event of a split, could demand custody or visitation rights and would be responsible for paying child support.

Asked why it was so important to recognize all three of them in the eyes of the law, Sharon responds, "When you look back on your life, there's a big difference between your father and your uncle and your parents' best friends. There are certain rights and responsibilities that also come with being a parent, and those rights and responsibilities only come with being a parent."

Third-parent adoptions remain extremely rare, and only a handful have been done, mostly in Massachusetts and California. But some legal scholars see in them the seeds of a larger shift in how the law defines parenthood. These advocates point to a few recent court decisions that suggest a willingness to recognize more than two parents.

The Laws Have Been Changed to Reflect Societal Change

It would not be the first time that American law has changed the rules of parenthood. According to Polikoff, in the English common law from which American law is derived, children born out of wedlock before the 19th century had, legally speaking, no parents at all. They were filius nullius [illegitimate]. By the 1800s, however, their status had changed—legal parentage was automatically assigned to the mother. If she was unmarried, she was the sole parent; if she was married, her husband was the father, regardless of whether he was biologically related.

In the 20th century, the most significant change in parenting law was erasing the distinction between legitimate and illegitimate children. Until the 1960s, the law regularly denied rights to children born out of wedlock: the right to collect workers' compensation benefits or Social Security survivor benefits for a dead parent, for example, or sue for a parent's wrongful death or inherit in the absence of a will (so-called intestate succession). With the sexual revolution, of course, popular attitudes about marriage changed, and the law changed with them. In decisions in 1968 and 1972, the Supreme Court struck down state statutes penalizing children born to unmarried mothers. The states claimed the laws encouraged marriage, but the justices focused on the fact that the penalties were largely aimed at the children.

Today's proponents of expanding the definition of parenthood argue that restricting the number of parents to two people also disadvantages children, at least those in certain nontraditional households. If a child grows up thinking of more than two people as parents, these lawyers and legal scholars argue, then the law should protect those relationships and the emotional connection and material support that come with them. Doing so may not be necessary as long as all of the parents get along and remain equally committed to the child—or children—but if the parents have a falling-out or if the custodial parents split up, then the people the law officially recognizes as parents hold all the cards, and can shut the others out of the child's life.

In addition, in the eyes of the law, a child doesn't have any claim on the financial resources of parental figures beyond the legally recognized two. The relationship is not unlike those of illegitimate children and their parents before 1968. With very few exceptions, it is today impossible for children to sue for child support, collect Social Security survivor benefits, or inherit by intestate succession from self-identified third or fourth parents, since the law doesn't recognize the relationship.

Some Argue That Children Are Punished If the Laws Are Not Changed

To critics of the legal status quo, all of this means that just as with illegitimacy laws, the courts are punishing children in the interest of preserving a traditional family structure, making their lives more uncertain by depriving them of emotional and financial support. . . .

Recognizing multiple fathers or multiple mothers, however, doesn't necessarily mean that they all have the same rights. In the Pennsylvania case [referring to a custody decision involving a biological mother, her same-sex partner, and a sperm donor], the court did not decide that all three parents had equal custody or were responsible for the same amount of child support. [Melanie] Jacobs [a law professor at Michgan State University] in particular has argued that expanding the number of legal parents a child has requires that courts begin to allow for degrees of legal parenthood, what she calls a scheme of "relative rights." Whereas today the law tends to see someone as either a parent or a nonparent, she argues that it should instead recognize gradations. For example, she argues, a known sperm donor should perhaps have certain parental rights and responsibilities—visitation and the obligation to pay some child support—but not the right to demand custody.

For critics, "disaggregating" the rights and responsibilities of parenthood, as Jacobs suggests, exposes a larger problem with the idea of expanding beyond two in the first place. Traditional legal definitions of parenthood, though they may not exactly correspond with every family's day-to-day reality, do lay out a set of hard and fast, inescapable obligations. If courts begin to experiment and innovate with what being a parent means, that may create uncertainty, and even a sense that parental obligations to children may be more negotiable than they once were.

June Carbone, a law professor at the University of Missouri-Kansas City, points to research Deirdre Bowen at Seattle University has done that suggests that in same-sex couples with a child, there's a great deal of ignorance and miscommunication about what the legal rights and responsibilities of each parent are.

"I think it is very important that there be a shaping of expectations at the outset," Carbone says.

Others Contend That Conflicts Will Increase as Well

Opponents of the change also worry that increasing the number of parents increases the odds of disagreements—over everything from where the child goes to school and what religion to raise him to how much time he spends with which parent—and the odds that those disagreements get litigated.

"Expanding the number of parents that would have rights to a child could, on the upside, expand the number of people who have responsibilities to that child, but it also expands the number of people who have a claim on that child, and who could come into conflict with the other parents," says Elizabeth Marquardt of the Institute for American Values, a nonprofit dedicated to encouraging traditional two-parent households. . . .

Some . . . changes [to the family] remain deeply controversial, of course. And yet there are other aspects of the contemporary family that, while they would strike people of an earlier era as deeply unnatural, today go all but unremarked: the fact, for example, that it's common for grandparents to live not with their children and grandchildren but instead hundreds of miles away. The family of the future may look similarly unfamiliar to us, and in ways we're only beginning to discern.

Periodical and Internet Sources Bibliography

The following articles have been selected to supplement the diverse views presented in this chapter.

| Angeline Acain | "Two Dads and a Dozen Children," *Gay Parent*, November/December 2010. |

Mackenzie Carpenter "What Happens to Kids Raised by Gay Parents?," *Pittsburgh Post-Gazette*, June 9, 2007.

Jessica Cerretani "I'm Coming Out: It Became a Test of Sorts—How Would Boyfriends React to My Dad Being Gay?," *Boston Globe*, October 18, 2009.

Mona Charen "Are Children of Gay Parents Worse Off?," Townhall.com, October 6, 2011.

Bob Ewegen "Tear Down Our Wall of Bigotry," *Denver Post*, March 10, 2007.

John Hoffman "Same-Sex Parenting: The Kids Are Alright," *Today's Parent*, July 2010.

Ann Hulbert "The Gay Science: What Do We Know About the Effects of Same-Sex Parenting?," *Slate*, March 12, 2004. www.slate.com.

Laura Laing "All in the Family: Kids Raised by Same-Sex Couples Speak Out to Defend Their Families," *Baltimore City Paper*, March 22, 2006.

Jay Leffew "Gay Parenting . . . Dealing in Honesty," *Gay Values*, February 18, 2010. http://open.salon.com.

Elizabeth Marquardt "The Revolution in Parenthood: The Emerging Global Clash Between Adult Rights and Children's Needs," AmericanValues.org, 2006.

Jim Spencer "Hypocrisy of Focus Ad All Too Clear," *Denver Post*, June 2, 2006.

OPPOSING
VIEWPOINTS®
SERIES

How Do Gay Families Impact Society?

Chapter Preface

The Defense of Marriage Act (DOMA) was signed into law by President Bill Clinton on September 21, 1996. As social conservatives grew concerned about gays and lesbians being given the right to legally marry in some states, DOMA was drafted to protect the institution of traditional marriage. It also defines marriage as a union between one man and one woman.

Under DOMA, states do not have to recognize gay couples who were married in other states that allow same-sex marriages. The act is meant to protect states against the full faith and credit clause of article 2, section 1 of the US Constitution that mandates that states must recognize the legislative acts and judicial decisions of other states. DOMA states: "No State, territory, or possession of the United States, or Indian tribe, shall be required to give effect to any public act, record, or judicial proceeding of any other State, territory, possession, or tribe respecting a relationship between persons of the same sex that is treated as a marriage under the laws of such other State, territory, possession, or tribe, or a right or claim arising from such relationship." This means that only legally married couples are eligible for federal marriage benefits, including Social Security payments paid to spouses.

On February 23, 2011, the President Barack Obama administration said that it would no longer defend DOMA because it "contains numerous expressions reflecting moral disapproval of gays and lesbians and their intimate and family relationships—precisely the kind of stereotype-based thinking and animus [animosity] the (Constitution's) Equal Protection Clause is designed to guard against," according to Attorney General Eric Holder.

On November 10, 2011, the Senate Judiciary Committee voted to rescind the law. The Democrats on the committee voted to repeal the law, while the Republicans voted to keep the law. It is not given a chance of being passed by the House of Representatives, in which the Republicans hold the majority of seats.

Supporters of DOMA believe that the law is needed because they believe that traditional marriage must be protected from gay and lesbian families. Tony Perkins, the president of the Family Research Council, said on July 20, 2011, "The Defense of Marriage Act reflects recognition of the uniquely important role that marriage between a man and a woman plays for society, in encouraging the reproduction of the human race and the joint nurture of children by the mother and father who produce them. DOMA has stood the test of time, being upheld as constitutional by several courts and successfully ensuring that federal law reflects our national consensus on marriage and that states will not have a radical redefinition of marriage forced upon them by other states."

Opponents argue that the Defense of Marriage Act discriminates against gays and lesbians and is unconstitutional because it prevents the federal government from acknowledging gay and lesbian marriages that were performed in states that do recognize such marriages. According to Marriage Equality USA, "DOMA violates constitutional protections that forbid the Government from discriminating by creating second-class citizens and second-class marriages."

Gay parenting continues to be a controversial issue as the number of gay couples starting families of their own continues to grow. In the following chapter, commentators offer their opinions on whether gay families change society for better or for worse, debate what constitutes a "traditional" family in today's society, and discuss the threat, if any, that gay families pose to religion.

"*The more gays are accepted as equal citizens, the more stable heterosexual marriage will become.*"

Gay Marriage Will Improve Society

Michael Alvear

In the following viewpoint, Michael Alvear argues that once gay marriage is accepted by society and made legal, heterosexual marriages will become more stable because there will be less pressure on gay individuals to marry heterosexuals. Alvear believes that it is not only the license for gays to marry that will benefit heterosexual marriage but also the shift in attitude regarding same-sex marriage that will result. He also notes that gay couples could provide loving homes for the many children in foster care. Michael Alvear is the author of Men Are Pigs, but We Love Bacon.

As you read, consider the following questions:

1. According to the viewpoint, what are some ways gay marriage will improve the lives of heterosexuals?

Michael Alvear, "Q: Would the Legalization of Gay Marriage Result in a Net Benefit to Heterosexuals? Yes: Divorce Rates Triggered by Fraudulent Marriages Will Go Down and More Children Will Grow Up in Stable Homes," *Insight on the News*, December 22, 2003. Reproduced by permission.

2. Why, according to Alvear, will heterosexual marriage become more stable when more gays are accepted as equal citizens?

3. As stated in the viewpoint, what drives gay men and women into fraudulent marriages?

As outrageous as it may sound, gay marriage will greatly improve the lives of heterosexuals. It will reduce the number of divorces caused by fraudulent marriages, ensure that more orphaned children grow up in stable and loving homes, raise the standard of living for children with gay parents, make neighborhoods safer for families and boost the economies of struggling communities.

It is not the license to marry that will create these benefits; it is the massive shift in attitude that will result from it. Allowing gays to marry will do to homophobia what civil rights legislation did for racism—reduce it substantially over the years.

The more gays are accepted as equal citizens, the more stable heterosexual marriage will become. Why? Because there are an untold number of traditional marriages that break up because one spouse comes out of the closet.

Homophobia and the Pressure to Conform

Homophobia drives gay men and women into fraudulent marriages. Pressure to conform, the weight of discrimination, potential loss of cherished dreams—serving in the military, worshipping in church, getting job promotions, raising kids—propels many into marriages to which they otherwise wouldn't commit.

Take my friend Cooper. Cooper is 64. He was married for 38 years. The divorce is pending. He leaves behind him a woman whose life was shattered by a truth that tunneled its way out of the mounds of shame, hostility and hatred that society heaped on it. Homophobia has a way of wounding gay and straight alike. It creates two classes of victims: people who are forced to lie and the people to whom they lie. As homophobia decreases, so will the pressure for gays and lesbians to enter into fig-leaf marriages—which, in turn, prevents children from being hurt by divorce and helps heterosexuals, such as Cooper's wife, create authentic, stable marriages.

Could gay marriage be a solution for the many children in foster care? There are plenty of gay and lesbian families willing to adopt some of the 568,000 kids languishing in institutions, but statutory bans and local judiciaries refusing to grant gay-adoption petitions impede them. According to the Evan B. Donaldson Adoption Institute's latest national survey, only 40 percent of public and private adoption agencies have placed children with gay adoptive parents. The same survey showed that a majority of childless gay men and women would like to become parents.

Would children in foster care be better off living in loving gay homes or institutions that shuffle them from one home to another until they reach 18 years of age and "age out" of the system? Ask the American Academy of Pediatrics, the Child Welfare League of America, the North American Council on Adoptable Children, the American Psychiatric Association, the American Psychological Association and the National Association of Social Workers. Their conclusion: Gay and lesbian homes would be good for many of these kids.

Benefits of Allowing Gays to Marry

What's the best way of making that happen? Giving gay couples automatic adoption rights. And the most effective way to do that? Allow them to marry. Gay marriage wouldn't just improve the lives of orphans; it also would improve the lives of children who have parents that happen to be gay.

Let's say two women with average incomes have a child together; we'll call him Billy. Because the women aren't allowed to marry, Billy doesn't get the financial and emotional safety nets other children get. For example, if Billy has a serious accident while his biological mother is away, the hospital can deny him the right to see his second parent, effectively torturing the child at the time of his greatest need. If Billy comes home to recuperate, the boss isn't legally obligated to provide sick leave to Billy's second parent, effectively preventing a child from being soothed by his nurturing parent. If Billy's biological mother dies, the surviving parent has no legal rights to Billy, effectively allowing the state to rip him from the arms of a loving mother and throw him into the foster care system. If Billy's parents separate, the departing parent is under no legal obligation to provide alimony or child support, effectively plunging Billy into poverty.

From his parents' inability to get joint health-, home- and auto-insurance policies to his own inability to access his second parent's Social Security survivor benefits, Billy suffers. Allowing same-sex marriage would eliminate the unfair penalties children have to bear. Ultimately, the greatest benefactors to gay marriage are children—more than 500,000 of them.

Half a million? Yes, and that may be underestimated. Face-to-face surveys show that 1 percent of people identify themselves as gay. But random telephone surveys, which give more anonymity, produce numbers around 3 percent or 4 percent of the population. And online surveys, which give the most anonymity, consistently show the number to be around 6 percent. If the range is somewhere between 1 and 6 percent of the population, let's split the difference and call it 3 percent. But remember, that figure represents only the people brave enough to identify themselves publicly.

Still, 3 percent of the total U.S. population of adults ages 18 and older (215,474,215) means there are 6,464,226 men and women who self-identify as gay. Apply that figure to a Kaiser Family Foundation study finding that 8 percent of self-identified gays and lesbians are parents or legal guardians of a live-in child younger than 18, and you come up with 517,138 gay and lesbian households with children.

This means there are more than half a million children growing up with same-sex parents. It also means half a million children growing up with serious disadvantages caused by the prohibition of same-sex marriage.

Affected by Homophobia

For every gay man and woman who gets punished by the legal system, there are mothers and fathers and brothers and sisters who bear witness to it. The fact is, 57.6 million people are either directly or indirectly affected by homophobia. Only 6.4 million, or 11 percent, are actually gay. That means 89 percent of the people affected by discrimination against gays are heterosexual. Consider these estimated numbers:

6.4 million gays and lesbians;

6.4 million siblings of gays and lesbians (assuming each gay person has one sibling);

12.8 million parents of gays and lesbians (assuming each parent is alive);

25.6 million grandparents (assuming two sets of living grandparents);

6.4 million uncles and aunts (assuming one per gay person);

Total: 57.6 million.

No matter how they feel about homosexuality, no parent wants to see their child hurt, no brother wants to see his sister in danger, no uncle wants to see his nephew suffer. One of the intangible costs of homophobia is the excruciating emotional pain felt by everyone related to the gay family member. Lessen homophobia, as gay marriage will, and you lessen the strain on millions of families.

It also turns out that gay couples bring with them economic boons to the larger community. Five years ago Ferndale, Mich.'s downtown was lined with abandoned buildings. Today, after years of courting gays to live and start businesses, it has a vacancy rate of less than 3 percent. Ferndale followed the theories in the best-selling book *The Rise of the Creative Class*. Civic leaders across the country pay more than $10,000 to hear the author, urban planner Richard Florida, talk about the best way to revitalize their communities. His thesis: If cities want to jump-start their economies they must attract the dominant economic group in America—people who think for a living (doctors, lawyers, scientists, engineers, entrepreneurs and computer programmers). Dubbing them the "creative class," Florida points out they're the most dominant economic group, making up nearly 30 percent of the workforce.

Florida produced a number of indexes measuring characteristics of successful cities. There's a high-tech index (ranking cities by the size of their software, electronics and engineering sectors) and an innovation index (ranking cities by the number of patents per capita). But one of Florida's most talked-about rankings is the gay index. He told Salon.com: "Gays are the canaries of the creative economy. Where gays are will be a community that has the underlying preconditions that attract the creative class of people. Gays tend to gravitate toward the types of places that will be attractive to many members of the creative class."

Florida, a professor at Carnegie Mellon University in Pittsburgh, boils it down to this: If you want economic growth, one of the things you must do is attract gays. Not because there are disproportionate numbers of gays in "thinking jobs" but because their presence signals the values to which the creative class is attracted: diversity, open-mindedness, variety, eccentricity.

Examples of Florida's theories: Minneapolis's Loring Park, Boston's Jamaica Plain, Chicago's Boystown, Atlanta's Midtown, Washington's Dupont Circle and Adams-Morgan. Though each has the reputation of being a "gay mecca," any demographer will tell you that the vast majority of residents are heterosexual.

Stabilizing Influence of Marriage

Marriage is a stabilizing influence on relationships and a platform for greater prosperity. The benefits of marriage would encourage gays and lesbians to take even more risks in distressed neighborhoods, turning them into places that attract the mostly heterosexual "creative class." The payoff to cities is clear: Encouraging stability and prosperity among gay and lesbian couples results in a bigger tax base that can be used to improve schools, streets and parks for its mostly heterosexual citizens.

Gay marriage won't just benefit same-sex couples; it will benefit everyone. It will reduce divorces by preventing sham marriages, provide homes to the orphaned, protect the children of gay parents and revitalize distressed communities. It's one of those queer ironies: Gay marriage will strengthen heterosexual families.

> "This is about putting the legal stamp of
> approval on homosexuality and impos-
> ing it with force throughout the various
> social and political institutions of a so-
> ciety that would never accept it other-
> wise."

Gay Families Are Changing Society for the Worse

Brian Camenker

In the following viewpoint, Brian Camenker states that society is being forced to accept same-sex marriage in every facet of life, including public schools, public health issues, businesses, and adoption. He argues that a minority of judges and lawmakers are unfairly making gay parents and families an everyday part of life even though society in general condones homosexuality. Camenker is the founder of MassResistance, a socially conservative group based in Massachusetts.

As you read, consider the following questions:

1. According to Camenker, why was the 2006 civil rights lawsuit, which was filed to force schools to notify parents when gay-related subjects were taught, dismissed?

Brian Camenker, "What Same-Sex 'Marriage' Has Done to Massachusetts: It's Far Worse than Most People Realize," www.massresistance.org, October 20, 2008, pp. 1–4. Reproduced by permission.

2. According to the author, what must all insurances in Massachusetts recognize?

3. What does the author mean when he writes that gay marriage "hangs over society like a hammer with the force of law"?

Anyone who thinks that same-sex "marriage" is a benign eccentricity which won't affect the average person should consider what it has done in Massachusetts. It's become a hammer to force the acceptance and normalization of homosexuality on everyone. And this train is moving fast. What has happened so far is only the beginning.

On November 18, 2003, the Massachusetts Supreme Judicial Court announced its *Goodridge* opinion [referring to *Goodridge v. Dept. of Public Health*], ruling that it was unconstitutional not to allow same-sex "marriage." Six months later, homosexual marriages began to be performed.

Parents Have Lost Control Over What Is Taught in School

The homosexual "marriage" onslaught in public schools across the state started soon after the November 2003 court decision.

At my own children's high school there was a school-wide assembly to celebrate same-sex "marriage" in early December 2003. It featured an array of speakers, including teachers at the school who announced that they would be "marrying" their same-sex partners and starting families either through adoption or artificial insemination. Literature on same-sex marriage—how it is now a normal part of society—was handed out to the students.

Within months it was brought into the middle schools. In September 2004, an 8th-grade teacher in Brookline, MA, told National Public Radio [NPR] that the marriage ruling had opened up the floodgates for teaching homosexuality. "In my mind, I know that, 'OK, this is legal now.' If somebody wants to challenge me, I'll say, 'Give me a break. It's legal now,'" she told NPR. She added that she now discusses gay sex with her students as explicitly as she desires. For example, she said she tells the kids that lesbians can have vaginal intercourse using sex toys.

By the following year it was in elementary school curricula. Kindergartners were given picture books telling them that same-sex couples are just another kind of family, like their own parents. In 2005, when David Parker of Lexington, MA—a parent of a kindergartner—strongly insisted on being notified when teachers were discussing homosexuality or transgenderism with his son, the school had him arrested and put in jail overnight.

Second graders at the same school were read a book, *King and King*, about two men who have a romance and marry each other, with a picture of them kissing. When parents Rob and Robin Wirthlin complained, they were told that the school had no obligation to notify them or allow them to opt out their child.

In 2006 the Parkers and Wirthlins filed a federal civil rights lawsuit to force the schools to notify parents and allow them to opt out their elementary school children when homosexual-related subjects were taught. The federal judges dismissed the case. The judges ruled that because same-sex marriage is legal in Massachusetts, the school actually had a duty to normalize homosexual relationships to children, and that schools have no obligation to notify parents or let them opt out their children! Acceptance of homosexuality had become a matter of good citizenship!

Think about that: Because same-sex marriage is "legal," a federal judge has ruled that the schools now have a *duty* to portray homosexual relationships as normal to children, despite what parents think or believe!

In 2006, in the elementary school where my daughter went to kindergarten, the *parents of a third grader were forced to take their child out of school because a man undergoing a sex-change operation and cross-dressing was being brought into class* to teach the children that there are now "different kinds of families." School officials told the mother that her complaints to the principal were considered "inappropriate behavior."

Libraries have also radically changed. School libraries across the state, from elementary school to high school, now have shelves of books to normalize homosexual behavior and the lifestyle in the minds of kids, some of them quite explicit and even pornographic. Parents' complaints are ignored or met with hostility.

Over the past year, homosexual groups have been using *taxpayer money* to distribute a large, slick hardcover *book celebrating homosexual marriage*, titled *Courting Equality*, into every school library in the state.

It's become commonplace in Massachusetts schools for teachers to prominently display photos of their same-sex "spouses" and occasionally bring them to school functions. Both high schools in my own town now have principals who are "married" to their same-sex partners, whom they bring to school and introduce to the students.

"Gay days" in schools are considered necessary to fight "intolerance" which may exist against same-sex relationships. Hundreds of high schools and even middle schools across the state now hold "gay, lesbian, bisexual, and transgender appreciation days." They "celebrate" homosexual marriage and move forward to other behaviors such as cross-dressing and transsexuality. In my own town, a school committee member recently announced that combating "homophobia" is now a top priority.

Once homosexuality is normalized, all boundaries begin to [break] down. The schools are already moving on to normalizing transgenderism (including cross-dressing and sex changes). The state-funded Commission on Gay, Lesbian, Bisexual and Transgender Youth includes leaders who are transsexuals.

Society Is Being Forced to Cater to Homosexuals

The commissioner of the Massachusetts Department of Public Health is "married" to another man. In 2007 he told a crowd of kids at a state-sponsored youth event that it's "wonderful being gay" and he wants to make sure there's enough HIV testing available for all of them.

Since homosexual marriage became "legal" the *rates of HIV/AIDS have gone up considerably in Massachusetts.* This year [2008] public funding to deal with HIV/AIDS has risen by $500,000. As the homosexual lobby group MassEquality wrote to their supporters after successfully persuading the legislature to spend that money: "With the rate of HIV infections rising dramatically in Massachusetts, it's clear the fight against AIDS is far from over."

Citing "the right to marry" as one of the "important challenges" in a place where "it's a great time to be gay," *the Massachusetts Department of Public Health helped produce* "Little Black Book—Queer in the 21st Century," a hideous work of obscene pornography [that] was given to kids at Brookline High School on April 30, 2005. Among other things, it gives "tips" to boys on how to perform oral sex on other males, masturbate other males, and how to "safely" have someone urinate on you for sexual pleasure. It also included a directory of bars in Boston where young men meet for anonymous sex.

Given the extreme dysfunctional nature of homosexual relationships, the Massachusetts legislature has felt the need to *spend more money every year to deal with skyrocketing homosexual domestic violence.* This year $350,000 was budgeted, up $100,000 from last year.

All insurances in Massachusetts must now recognize same-sex "married" couples in their coverage. This includes auto insurance, health insurance, life insurance, etc.

Businesses must recognize same-sex "married" couples in *all their benefits, activities, etc.,* regarding both employees and customers.

The wedding industry is required [to] serve the homosexual community if requested. Wedding photographers, halls, caterers, etc., must do same-sex marriages or be arrested for discrimination.

Businesses are often "tested" for tolerance by homosexual activists. Groups of homosexual activists often go into restaurants or bars and publicly kiss and fondle each other to test whether the establishment demonstrates sufficient "equality"—now that homosexual marriage is "legal." In fact, more and more overt displays of homosexual affection are seen in public places across the state to reinforce "marriage equality."

The Massachusetts bar exam now tests lawyers on their knowledge of same-sex "marriage" issues. In 2007, a Boston man, Stephen Dunne, failed the Massachusetts bar exam because he refused to answer the questions in it about homosexual marriage.

Issues regarding homosexual "families" are now firmly entrenched in the Massachusetts legal system. In many firms, lawyers in Massachusetts practicing family law *must now attend seminars on homosexual "marriage."* There are also now several homosexual judges overseeing the Massachusetts family courts.

Gay Couples Are Being Given Preference in Adoption Cases

Homosexual "married" couples can now demand to be able to adopt children the same as normal couples. Catholic Charities decided to abandon handling adoptions rather [than] submit to regulations requiring them to allow homosexuals to adopt the children in their care.

In 2006 the Massachusetts Department of Social Services (DSS) honored two men "married" to each other as their "Par-

ents of the Year." The men already adopted a baby through DSS (against the wishes of the baby's birth parents). According to news reports, the day after that adoption was final DSS approached the men about adopting a second child. Homosexuals now appear to be put in line for adopting children ahead of heterosexual parents by state agencies in Massachusetts.

In 2004, Governor Mitt Romney ordered justices of the peace to perform homosexual marriages when requested or be fired. At least one justice of the peace decided to resign.

Also *marriage licenses in Massachusetts now have "Party A and Party B" instead of "husband and wife."* Imagine having a marriage license like that.

Since homosexual relationships are now officially "normal," *the legislature now gives enormous tax money to homosexual activist groups.* In particular, the Massachusetts Commission on Gay, Lesbian, Bisexual and Transgender Youth is made up of the most radical and militant homosexual groups [that] target children in the schools. This year they are getting $700,000 of taxpayer money to go into the public schools.

In 2008 Massachusetts changed the state Medicare laws to include homosexual "married" couples in the coverage.

Since gay "marriage," *annual gay pride parades* have become more prominent. There are more politicians and corporations participating, and even police organizations take part. *And the envelope gets pushed further and further.* There is now a profane "Dyke March" through downtown Boston, and recently a "transgender" parade in Northampton that included bare-chested women who have had their breasts surgically removed so they could "become" men. Governor [Deval] Patrick even marched with his "out lesbian" 17-year-old daughter in the 2008 Boston Pride event, right behind a "leather" group brandishing a black & blue flag, whips and chains!

The Media Favor Gay Couples

Boston media, particularly the *Boston Globe* newspaper, regularly does *feature stories and news stories portraying homosexual "married" couples where regular married couples would normally be used.* It's "equal," they insist, so there must be no difference in the coverage. Also, the *newspaper advice columns* now deal with homosexual "marriage" issues, and how to properly accept it.

A growing number of news reporters and TV anchors are openly "married" homosexuals who march in the "gay pride" parades.

The Future Is Being Decided
by a Few People

Homosexual "marriage" hangs over society like a hammer with the force of law. And it's only just begun. Unfortunately, like elsewhere in America, the imposition of same-sex marriage on the people of Massachusetts was a combination of radical, arrogant judges and pitifully cowardly politicians.

It's pretty clear that the homosexual movement's obsession with marriage is not because large numbers of them actually want to marry each other. In fact, a very low percentage of homosexuals actually "marry." (In fact, over the last three months, the Sunday *Boston Globe*'s marriage section hasn't had any photos of homosexual marriages. In the beginning it was full of them.) Research shows that homosexual relationships are fundamentally dysfunctional on many levels, and "marriage" as we know it isn't something they can achieve, or even desire. This is about putting the legal stamp of approval on homosexuality and imposing it with force throughout the various social and political institutions of a society that would never accept it otherwise. To the rest of America: You've been forewarned.

> *"Some research shows that benefits to children of traditional family structures have generally compared two-parent situations with children being raised by single parents."*

Gay Families Are the Same as Traditional Families

Rich Mkhondo

In the following viewpoint, Rich Mkhondo discusses the religious criticism of gay marriage. Many Christians and religious followers alike cite multiple biblical passages "banning" gay marriage. Mkhondo claims that many people pick which biblical passages to obey and which to ignore. He also notes that there is not much research comparing same-sex homes with traditional homes; however, the data that is available shows children do just as well when they live with same-sex parents. Rich Mkhondo is a marketing and communications executive.

As you read, consider the following questions:

1. According to the viewpoint, what do opponents of same-sex marriage claim is their intent?

Rich Mkhondo, "Let Gays, Lesbians Get Hitched; Those Who Oppose Same-Sex Unions Refer to the Biblical Tradition to Deny People Their Freedom," *The Star* (South Africa), November 28, 2006. Reproduced by permission.

2. About what do critics of gay marriage claim a child of same-sex couples is liable to be confused?

3. As stated in the viewpoint, do arguments against same-sex marriage rest on religious or legal principles?

Love, sex, money, law, politics, religion, culture and what's best for the children. These were hot-button issues raised during the debate leading to the passage of the civil union bill, which could see South Africa becoming the first country in Africa to recognise same-sex marriage.

Bravo to those politicians and fellow South Africans who recognise that marriage is not a special right or commodity; nor an exclusive club that should be closed to some citizens.

It is a fundamental right that must be available to all. The benefits of marriage, which are conferred by society to honour the love and commitment of two people, cannot be justly withheld from certain citizens and afforded to others.

It's sad that the public, our constitution and parliament have had to be dragged into the debate about same-sex marriage. This has been made necessary by the arrogance of those who believe that same-sex marriage is an assault on the very meaning of the word.

Opponents of same-sex marriage say their intent is not to discriminate but to defend the tradition of the man-woman union (Peter and Patricia), which is older than any government and more fundamental to human society than any written law.

Sacrament Defined by God

For the opponents, marriage is a sacrament, defined by God as a union between a man and a woman, who pledge to be faithful, to procreate, and to stay together in order to raise the children and to honour the institution itself.

For the critics of Peter marrying Paul or Margaret tying the knot with Maria, the historical norms of marriage are under assault from many directions, including divorce, infidelity and cohabitation without marriage. But to change the essential nature of marriage by opening it up to same-sex couples would alter it radically and damage it.

They say that God's plan for marriage to be between one man and one woman is reflected in the Bible. The King James Version refers to sex between two men as an abomination (Leviticus) and as something that will keep practitioners from inheriting the kingdom of God (First Corinthians). The Scriptures do not explicitly address gay or lesbian marriage because, they say, until recently it was utterly unthinkable.

There are even those who go further and say research has shown that a stable family with a father and mother in the home is the best circumstance in which to raise children. Children who are raised by parents of the same sex are liable to be confused about the natural order of sexuality.

So, the critics are defending what they regard as the most fundamental building block of society, the concept of a family made up of one man, one woman and their children; marriage between a man and woman is a concept deeply rooted in history, tradition and the Bible.

Religiously, those who support same-sex marriage respond in several ways to the biblical texts cited. They challenge the translation and raise the historical context of passages in Leviticus, Romans and Corinthians that lead some readers to believe that gays are condemned.

They note that the same passage of Leviticus that criticises sex between two men also bans sex with a woman during her menstrual cycle.

Picking Which Passages to Obey

People pick biblical passages to obey and others to disregard. The Bible, some pastors say, is not a rule book, and we use the power of the Holy Spirit and the risen Lord Jesus Christ to figure things out. The Holy Spirit guides people to believe that monogamy is to be supported and that couples seeking to create loving, committed, monogamous relationships are to be welcomed.

Some research shows that benefits to children of traditional family structures have generally compared two-parent situations with children being raised by single parents. Less data is available comparing children raised by two same-sex parents, but research mostly shows that such children do as well in school and in their emotional well-being.

For me, it is important to recognise that the so-called traditional elements of marriage have changed to reflect the ideal of individual equality under the law. So, securing same-sex marriage is, quite simply, another advance in the struggle to extend to all South African citizens the equal right to enter into a contract with their life partner of choice.

Indeed, arguments against same-sex marriage usually focus on the sanctity of marriage as a procreative union between a man and a woman. [To] those who argue that marriage is the single most important stabilising foundation in our society because it creates long-lasting relationships and thereby strengthens and builds the community [we ask], if marriage is such a stabilising influence, why should we exclude some people from its domain?

When people say they believe in the sanctity of marriage, this assumes that the marriage relationship has been static since time began. But this isn't the case. Initially, married women were treated as chattel owned and controlled by their husbands.

Likewise, apartheid rulers prohibited interracial marriages. History books teach us that hundreds of years ago, divorces didn't exist, and the dissolution of marriage was much more difficult to obtain and carried a great stigma, especially for women.

Gay Families and Traditional Families Are Not Really All That Different

Acceptance of sexual and gender diversity does not threaten civilization as we know it, or the family and traditional religion. Sure, some gay people are wild and crazy, while others are boring and dull—just like straight people. Whatever your approach to sexuality, whether you are a family man or a playboy, you will find gay people who live like you do. The gay/straight "line" just has nothing to do with sexual morality—or with raising healthy children for that matter.

Jay Michaelson,
"Dispelling the Myth of God Versus Gay,"
USA Today, *November 2011.*

Resting on Religious Principles

Also, arguments against same-sex marriage usually rest on religious rather than legal principles.

Civil marriages have always existed outside of and apart from marital unions receiving the blessing of any religious institution.

Today many religions openly support gay and lesbian marriage and regularly perform commitment ceremonies, proof that any foundation for a unified religious objection to same-sex marriage is slipping away.

Also, religion and civil marriage are two distinctly separate things. Surely parliament should not have the right to dictate for whom religious bodies may perform marriage services— just as religious institutions shouldn't dictate who may obtain a civil marriage license from the government.

Surely same-sex couples are more similar to their heterosexual counterparts than they are different?

Regardless of sex, race, religion, or national origin, there are the day-to-day worries about paying the mortgage and what to make for dinner. Same-sex couples face the same questions about how to raise children and how to prepare for retirement.

Legal Protections

So why can't same-sex couples have the legal protections or benefits that accompany civil marriage?

If they take responsibility for their partner's well-being—both economically and emotionally—why should same-sex couples be legally treated as nothing more than roommates?

Legal marriage is a civil contract between two people that provides certain rights and imposes certain obligations.

What possible justification can there be for denying this basic civil right to a few million same-sex couples?

Surely most human beings at some point in their lives desire to share their fortunes and misfortunes with a partner with whom they have formed lasting bonds, desire to provide emotional stability and economic security for their loved ones, desire to feel secure in the knowledge that their loved ones' emotional and economic security are protected by law.

Some also desire to raise a family. In this respect, as in many others, gays and lesbians are no different from heterosexuals.

Discriminating against gays and lesbians by claiming their decision to love each other and make a personal commitment is somehow bad for society and a threat to marriage is discrimination born of ignorance and founded on fear.

Same-sex marriage in South Africa should not be about the right to choose a certain lifestyle.

It should be about offering the same rights and civil liberties to all citizens without discrimination.

The question is not whether or not our country needs or is ready for same-sex marriage.

The question is why gay and lesbian couples should have to wait any longer for their civil rights.

The civil union bill and therefore same-sex marriage is clearly about legal protection under the law, regardless of whether it conflicts with personal religious beliefs, cultures or upbringing.

Same-sex marriage is not about a lifestyle. It's about equal rights and civil liberties, beliefs in which our democracy was founded, and which we can't ignore.

> "Men and women still compose the two great halves of humanity. Men and women are still wonderfully and uniquely different, and men and women still play important and irreplaceable roles in the family."

Gay Families Can Never Be the Same as Traditional Families

Austin R. Nimocks

In the following viewpoint, Austin R. Nimocks argues that marriage always has been accepted throughout the world as one of the basic foundations of society. He contends that a major reason for marriage is procreation, and he is critical of those who would redefine marriage to include same-sex relationships. He maintains that a mother and a father cannot be replaced because each one has such an integral role to play in a family. Nimocks is senior legal counsel for the Alliance Defense Fund, which is dedicated to protecting and preserving religious liberty and the sanctity of life, marriage, and the family.

As you read, consider the following questions:

1. According to Nimocks, what is "a key purpose of marriage"?

2. As the author outlines, what determines due process rights?

3. According to the author, what was decided in *Loving v. Virginia*?

As debates currently rage about budget deficits, debt ceilings, and jobs, I am pleased that the Senate is discussing what are arguably the two most important jobs in our society—the jobs of mothers and fathers. The Defense of Marriage Act (DOMA) gives us a chance to think about the roles of mothers and fathers in our society, and also to consider a question often overlooked in these debates: Why is government in the marriage business?

Congress enacted DOMA in 1996 by an 84% margin, demonstrating broad bipartisan support. When it did so, Congress stated that "at bottom, civil society has an interest in maintaining and protecting the institution of heterosexual marriage because it has a deep and abiding interest in encouraging responsible procreation and child rearing. Simply put, government has an interest in marriage because it has an interest in children." This statement still holds true. As evidenced by the most extensive national research survey on Americans' attitudes about marriage, 62% of Americans agree that "marriage should be defined only as a union between one man and one woman."

Traditional Families Are the Cornerstone of Society

What DOMA addresses is not just a law or creature of statute, but a social institution that has universally crossed all political, religious, sociological, geographical, and historical lines.

As the philosopher and self-described atheist Bertrand Russell wrote, "But for children, there would be no need of any institution concerned with sex." He continued, "It is through children alone that sexual relations become of importance to society, and worthy to be taken cognizance of by a legal institution." Renowned anthropologist Claude Lévi-Strauss observed that "the family—based on a union, more or less durable, but socially approved, of two individuals of opposite sexes who establish a household and bear and raise children—appears to be a practically universal phenomenon, present in every type of society."

From lexicographers who have defined marriage, to academic scholars who have explained marriage, to legislatures and courts that have legally recognized marriage, all demonstrate that a key purpose of marriage is to benefit society by procreative relationships. Marriage between a man and a woman is a long-standing, worldwide institution that is a building block of society.

Marriage doesn't proscribe conduct or prevent individuals from living how they want to live. It doesn't prohibit intimate relationships or curtail one's constitutional rights. Federal legislation that protects marriage as a binding, exclusive, and procreative relationship has the public purposes of marriage—most notably, to continue human existence—at heart. The effort to repeal DOMA, however, tries to replace these essential public purposes of marriage with various private purposes. Our discussion of DOMA and its repeal should not be about the *private* reasons why individuals marry, why the institution of marriage benefits any particular couple, or why any two people should or should not marry. Instead, we must speak about social policy for our country as a whole and the government's interest in marriage as an institution.

Due to the public nature of the government's interest in marriage, a couple's entrance into marriage has never been conditioned on the couple's ability and desire to find happiness together, on their level of financial entanglement, or on their actual personal dedication to each other. Because the scope of due process rights is determined not by anyone's individual circumstances, but by the country's history, traditions, and legal practices, marriage laws stem from the fact that children are the natural product of sexual relationships between men and women, and that both fathers and mothers are viewed to be necessary and important for children. Thus, throughout history, diverse cultures and faiths have recognized marriage between one man and one woman as the best way to promote healthy families and societies.

There Are Roles That Only a Man and a Woman Can Fill

Moreover, studies and data from the social sciences have long demonstrated that for children, the ideal family structure is one headed by two opposite-sex biological parents in a low-conflict marriage. Even President [Barack] Obama supports active and involved fatherhood for all children; he knows all too well the pain of not having a father during his childhood, even though he was raised by a loving mother. As he stated:

> We know the statistics—that children who grow up without a father are five times more likely to live in poverty and commit crime; nine times more likely to drop out of schools and twenty times more likely to end up in prison. They are more likely to have behavioral problems, or run away from home, or become teenage parents themselves. And the foundations of our community are weaker because of it.

Likewise, a child psychologist who testified in support of a lawsuit that would judicially impose same-sex marriage on California citizens wrote, "Both mothers and fathers play crucial and qualitatively different roles in the socialization of the child."

But advocates for redefining marriage are asking you to cast aside the natural attachment of parents to their own children, and the natural desires of children to know who they are and where they came from. These advocates are asking the whole of society to ignore the unique and demonstrable differences between men and women in parenthood: no mothers, no fathers, just generic parents.

But there are no generic people. We are composed of two complementary, but different, halves of humanity. As Rutgers University sociologist David Popenoe puts it,

> We should disavow the notion that "mommies can make good daddies," just as we should disavow the popular notion ... that "daddies can make good mommies.". . . The two sexes are different to the core, and each is necessary—culturally and biologically—for the optimal development of a human being.

The Courts Have Ruled Against Same-Sex Marriage

The Senate should also disavow the idea that since the Obama administration refused to defend DOMA, its repeal is somehow a constitutional mandate. In 1967, the Supreme Court decided the case of *Loving v. Virginia.* In the *Loving* case, the Supreme Court struck down as unconstitutional a race-based marriage law that prohibited whites from marrying anyone of color. In so ruling, the Supreme Court called marriage "fundamental to our very existence and survival," because of its procreative aspects. The procreative nature of marriage is what brought about miscegenation laws in the first place. The court's ruling returned marriage in the United States to its original status in common law—an institution not to be manipulated by racial prejudice, but to be honored as the union of one man and one woman.

Those who push for redefining marriage often cite *Loving* to support their arguments. But in doing this, they miss the court's link between marriage and procreation. Even the De-

Traditional Families Are the Foundation of Society

One of the primary tenets upon which this organization [Citizens for Community Values] was established is the Judeo-Christian teaching that the family is the cornerstone of civilization. Inseparably linked to that tenet is the belief that marriage—i.e., one woman and one man living together in a lifelong, monogamous, covenantal relationship—is the foundational element of the family unit. Compromise the integrity of the marriage relationship, and you compromise the integrity of the family.

Some have reasoned that this "Judeo-Christian" teaching is based upon tradition, and that as the needs of societies change, adherence to tradition alone should not prevent us from adapting our traditions to changing needs and mores. But this teaching is grounded in more than tradition. This teaching is grounded in Scripture, and the truths of Scripture are absolute and are not subject to change.

"Where Do We Stand?,"
Citizens for Community Values, 2011. www.ccv.org.

partment of Justice, in its new refusal to defend DOMA, does not cite the *Loving* case as support for its new anti-marriage position.

Same-sex marriage supporters also routinely overlook a noteworthy court case argued and decided in 1972, five years after the *Loving* decision. The Supreme Court dismissed an appeal from the Minnesota Supreme Court that claimed an alternate definition of marriage was a basic human right. In *Baker v. Nelson*, the Minnesota Supreme Court rejected claims for same-sex marriage and held that "in common sense and in constitutional sense, there is a clear distinction between marital restriction based merely upon race and one based upon the fundamental difference in sex." The court's rejection also emphasized a defining link between marriage and "the procreation and rearing of children." The United States Supreme Court upheld the Minnesota court's decision. Not a single justice of the United States Supreme Court found the constitutional claims for an alternate definition of marriage substantial enough even to warrant a review.

Since the *Baker* case, every appellate court in this country, both state and federal, that has addressed the validity of marriage as the union of one man and one woman, under the United States Constitution, has upheld the institution as rationally related to the state's interest in responsible procreation and child rearing. And while some may argue that times have changed, they cannot credibly argue that humanity, as a gendered species, has changed. Men and women still compose the two great halves of humanity. Men and women are still wonderfully and uniquely different, and men and women still play important and irreplaceable roles in the family. As stated by the Supreme Court, "The truth is that the two sexes are not fungible; a community made up exclusively of one is different from a community composed of both; the subtle interplay of influence one on the other is among the imponderables." "'Inherent differences' between men and women, we have come to appreciate, remain cause for celebration."

Without question, the overwhelming majority of people *on both sides* of this debate are good and decent Americans, coming from all walks of life, all political parties, all races and creeds—but humanity remains unchanged as a collection of men and women. And since it will always be true that children are the product of sexual relationships between men and women, and that men and women each bring something distinctive to the table of parenting, this government maintains a compelling interest in protecting and preserving the institution of marriage as the union of one man and one woman. Marriage between a man and a woman naturally builds families—mom, dad, and children—and gives hope that the next generations will carry that family into the future.

> *"With the institution of marriage under assault from several directions, the concerted efforts of the Left are directed toward either keeping marriage from leading to families, or creating mockeries of marriage."*

Gay Families Are a Threat to Religion

James Heiser

In the following viewpoint, James Heiser asserts that same-sex marriage and gay families violate the teachings of Christianity. He contends that both present a threat to religious freedom because they weaken the traditional concept of marriage. Heiser is a reverend, the publisher of Repristination Press, and the author of several books, including A Shining City on a Higher Hill: Christianity and the Next New World.

As you read, consider the following questions:

1. According to Bradford Wilcox, in what segment of the population is marriage in the most trouble?

2. In the author's view, what two changes in President Obama's policies represent "an assault on the family"?

James Heiser, "Archbishop Protests Obama's Anti-Marriage Agenda," *The New American*, September 30, 2011. Reproduced by permission.

3. According to Heiser, what effect does the "religious exemption" clause have on Roman Catholic health care providers?

As the Obama administration continues the efforts of the radical Left to redefine terms such as "marriage" and "family" to the point where they have been emptied of their historic meaning, traditionalists are becoming increasingly vocal. New York Archbishop Timothy Dolan's September 26 talk—"The Ring Makes the Difference"—is one of the most prominent statements in opposition to such efforts at undermining the historic, traditional understanding of marriage. The archbishop denounced the effort to "redefine" marriage, declaring the effort to promulgate the notion of "same-sex" marriage as an "ominous threat to religious liberty."

Archbishop Dolan spoke this past Monday as part of a panel discussion in Poughkeepsie, and an article for the *Poughkeepsie Journal* reported that Dolan and other speakers emphasized the threat which "same-sex marriage" poses to the country:

> Dolan framed criticism aimed at the Catholic Church and opponents of same-sex marriage as an "ominous threat to religious liberty," warning of what he called "aggressive secularism."

> He said, "America needs and depends upon a vigorous free exercise of religion."

> Dolan placed his hand on his chest.

> "We need to recapture the awe, the wonder, the dignity of marriage," he said. "For many of our people, marriage has lost its luster."

> Dolan's point was driven home by Bradford Wilcox, director of the National Marriage Project at the University of Virginia, whose presentation included statistics from the 2010

study "The State of Our Unions: Marriage in America" jointly published by the National Marriage Project at the University of Virginia and the Center for Marriage and Families at the Institute for American Values.

"Marriage is most in trouble in middle American groups and the poor," he said, gesturing to a bar graph that showed 46 percent of marriages ended within the first 10 years among poor families.

An assault on the family—including repeal of the military's "don't ask, don't tell" policy and abandonment of the Defense of Marriage Act (DOMA)—has been a fundamental element of the policies of the Obama administration. As Daniel Sayani wrote for the *New American* in February of this year:

> While the Obama administration's decision to stop defending marriage as existing between one man and one woman indicates a break with its former policy on the issue, a closer analysis shows that President Obama has a long history of gay/lesbian activism, unconstitutionally usurping traditional definitions of the family.

Marriage is not the only "family" issue suffering a frontal assault by the Obama administration. The U.S. Conference of Catholic Bishops (USCCB) recently took the extraordinary step of issuing a very strongly worded statement in response to efforts by the Department of Health and Human Services (HHS) to strip any meaningful "religious exemption" clause from implementation of "Obamacare." As reported earlier this week for the *New American*, the USCCB found that HHS policy would attempt to coerce Roman Catholic health care providers to violate the teachings of their church by requiring them to provide abortions, abortifacient drugs, and contraceptives.

With the institution of marriage under assault from several directions, the concerted efforts of the Left are directed toward either keeping marriage from leading to families, or

Judeo-Christian Values Are Being Disregarded

Since the secular age began, the notion that one should look to religion—or to any past wisdom—for one's values has died. Thus, the modern attempts to undo the Judeo-Christian value system as the basis of America's values [is] to disparage the Founders as essentially morally flawed individuals (They allowed slavery, didn't they?).

Dennis Prager,
"California Decision Will Radically Change Society,"
Dennisprager.com, May 20, 2008.

creating mockeries of marriage which are, by definition, barren. With the administration waging war on marriage, Archbishop Dolan responded to the president's actions in the strongest possible terms; according to CNSNews.com, he declared that President Obama's actions were, in fact, a threat not only to families, but to church and state as well. In Dolan's words:

> Thus, the comprehensive efforts of the federal government—using its formidable moral, economic, and coercive power—to enforce its new legal definition of 'marriage' against a resistant church would, if not reversed, precipitate a systemic national conflict between church and state, harming both institutions, as well as our Nation as a whole. . . .

Far from the administration responding to such concerns regarding the fundamental institutions that uphold the Republic, CNSNews' Terence Jeffrey explains that it appears Mr. Obama actually went even further in his assault on marriage in the aftermath of the recent rebukes from the Roman Catholic Church:

In his letter last week to the president about the marriage issue, Archbishop Dolan indicated that the only "response" he and Cardinal George had received from their previous communications was a stepped up attack on marriage by the administration.

"This past spring the Justice Department announced that it would no longer defend the Defense of Marriage Act (DOMA) in court, a decision strongly opposed by the Catholic Bishops of the United States and many others," the archbishop told the president.

"Now the Justice Department has shifted from not defending DOMA—which is problem enough, given the duty of the executive branch to enforce even laws it disfavors—to actively attacking DOMA's constitutionality," the archbishop said.

No doubt a fight with the Roman Catholic Church would play well with large elements of Mr. Obama's "base" of political support, since anything he could do to anger traditionalists and social conservatives would please many of those who are funding his bid for reelection. Perversely, Mr. Obama has much to gain from inflicting losses on the fundamental fabric of American society; the agenda he has pursued to date has waged war on the religious principles of his opponents, and he shows little sign of an interest in doing otherwise. While the political elites attack the roots of civilization—roots which are sunk deep into the church, the state and the home—those who would seek to defend the framework of human society can readily attest to the devastation which has been wrought upon those roots in recent years.

> *"The effort to deny equality to members of society on shifting religious grounds and nonexistent practical ones is a war on decency as well as on conservative sense."*

Gay Families Are Not a Threat to Religion

Douglas Murray

In the following viewpoint, Douglas Murray maintains that gay marriage is not a threat to religion and should be welcomed by conservatives. He argues that the fact that gays and lesbians want to marry shows that they value the importance of marriage and commitment. Murray contends that gay marriage might encourage more people—both gay and straight—to marry and discourage promiscuity. Murray, a writer and commentator, is an associate director of the Henry Jackson Society.

As you read, consider the following questions:

1. In Murray's view, how can interpreting the Bible be a problem when debating gay marriage?

2. According to Murray, what should be "quid pro quo"?

3. What part of the population does conservative politician Paul Goodman say must be included for equal representation of opinions on the issue?

Gay marriage will never jeopardize straight marriage. But it can provoke political divorce.

In America a new generation of Republicans is challenging the traditional consensus of their party on gay marriage. They—as well as some of the GOP old guard like Dick Cheney—are coming out in favour. In Britain the subject is also back on the agenda with the coalition government, at the insistence of the prime minister apparently, planning a 'public consultation' on the matter.

Though not exactly political leadership, this nevertheless constitutes a change—not least in stealing the mantle of gay equality from the Left. For decades it was presumed that conservatives could only oppose such moves. But as young Republicans like Margaret Hoover (author of *American Individualism*) are showing, that needn't be the case.

Indeed the best arguments for gay marriage are conservative ones.

But first there are the non-arguments.

Among them are those claiming that giving gays the right to marry somehow destabilises heterosexual marriage. But divorce and adultery are the biggest under-miners of marriage. Has any man abandoned his wife because of gay marriage? Then there is the slippery-slope argument. Tory MP Edward Leigh worries that if gays are allowed to marry, 'There is no logical reason why the new alternative institution should be limited to two people. Why not three?' he asks.

'Or 33?' All of which tells us more about his imagination than his logic.

Few sights in politics are quite as risible as the male politician in full, puffing flight from an issue of basic gay equality. As the campaigning lawyer Elizabeth Birch said when arguing with the three-times-married conservative representative Bob Barr in 1990, 'Which marriage are you defending? Your first, your second or your third?'

The idea that marriage is solely for the procreation of children is equally dismissible. Plenty of straight couples, particularly older ones, do not marry to have children.

They marry to form a deep, committed and publicly respected bond. In any case, if protecting the special nature of marriage were the true drive of anti-equality activists, then they might focus instead on those celebrity and 'reality' stars who transparently marry for the publicity. Perhaps campaigners should picket Katie Price's weddings?

But true conservatives should welcome gay marriage. For its increasing acceptance across civilised countries represents not the making gay of marriage but the making conservative of gays. The desire of an increasing number of gay men and women to have their stable and lifelong relationships recognised equally by family, friends and society as a whole demonstrates the respect of individuals within, and towards, an important institution.

Those who fear or dislike perceived aspects of gay life should particularly welcome gay acceptance into the marital fold.

An aspect of male 'gay life' some heterosexuals claim to have a problem with is the perceived promiscuity. Whether this is in reality any more distinctive than among straight people, gay marriage offers a remedy, giving gays, like straights, a public and private path towards commitment. At a time when many heterosexuals are spurning the idea of marriage, here is a section of society positively lobbying for the right to respect and continue the institution. Perhaps gay marriage will encourage more straight people back on to the marital path?

Of course the argument most commonly made against gay marriage is the worst of all: the religious argument. Ignoring

Religious Should Be Accepting of Everyone

If I'm right, [gospel writer] Luke's Jesus is against every-thing that ranks and separates God's people. If I'm right, Luke's Jesus would be appalled at the ways in which God's people are ranked and separated according to their sexual orientation, their gender identity, their marital status and even more appalled at the ways in which God's people are ranked and separated according to the sexual orientation, the gender identity, and the marital status of their parents and their children.

Fintan Moore,
"Gathered Around Him Was a Great Crowd,"
Institute for Welcoming Resources, February 11, 2007.
www.welcomingresources.org.

for a moment whether anyone really wishes to reinstate the practice of consulting 'holy books' for the specifics of lawmak-ing, the lack of consistency is extraordinary. A few months back I found myself debating a lady from the General Synod. The presence of a verse in the book of Leviticus was her justi-fication for arguing against any rights for gays. 'What about the imprecations against all sorts of dietary laws in the same book?' I asked her. 'What of the warning against the mixing of fabrics? What about that verse in Exodus, "Thou shalt not suf-fer a witch to live?"' 'Well, I don't know anything about that,' she said. Citing scriptural authority raises not only problems of source, but problems with the reading of a verse.

Nonetheless, if gays are allowed to marry there should be give and take. Marriage equality should not be forced on reli-gious institutions. Religious people of all denominations might keep making the argument within their faiths. But there is no more justification in the religious being forced to accept things they claim to be against their beliefs than there is in the religious forcing their beliefs on everyone else. That should be the quid pro quo. If the religious want to enjoy freedom from the secular, then the secular should be able to enjoy freedom from the religious. But the reasons for denying basic equality on religious grounds is not only inconsistent, it has become desperate.

Some people will seize any boomerang they can to resist the case.

For instance, in 2004 the former Conservative MP Paul Goodman voted against the introduction even of the halfway house of civil partnerships, fearing their introduction would 'compromise an institution which is an integral feature of our social ecology'. Mr Goodman, now executive editor of Conservative Home, is a married convert to Catholicism. Six years on from the Civil Partnership Act becoming law, there is no word on whether it has compromised the 'social ecology' of his own marriage. But like so many other opponents of equal rights, he has now shifted his case. This time around, in opposing the government's equal-marriage proposals, he cites among other things the importance of canvassing Muslim opinion in any plan for equality. To call this disingenuous is to state the situation too generously.

The religious case against equal rights can—and probably will—be argued till the end of time. But the effort to deny equality to members of society on shifting religious grounds and nonexistent practical ones is a war on decency as well as on conservative sense. The government should lead the way against this, not with a drawn-out consultation but a clear demonstration of what belongs to the secular state and what belongs to the religious conscience. Future generations of married people, straight and gay, will thank them for it.

Periodical and Internet Sources Bibliography

The following articles have been selected to supplement the diverse views presented in this chapter.

Benjamin Anastas   "O Pioneers!," *New York Times*, November 4, 2011.

Nicholas P. Cafardi   "Civil Marriage Is for Caesar to Decide, Not the Church," *National Catholic Reporter*, July 5, 2011.

Linda Carroll   "Gay Families More Accepted than Single Moms," MSNBC, March 15, 2011. www.msnbc.com.

Joan Chittister   "Whatever Happened to the Middle?," *National Catholic Reporter*, May 26, 2010.

Commonweal   "Protecting Religious Freedom," August 12, 2011.

Stephanie Coontz   "Gay Marriage Isn't Revolutionary. It's Just Next," *Washington Post*, January 9, 2011.

Petula Dvorak   "Bert and Ernie Are the Wrong Guys for This Mission," *Washington Post*, August 12, 2011.

Thomas C. Fox   "Boulder Parents: Adult Child of Gay Parents Speaks from Experience," *National Catholic Reporter*, March 26, 2010.

Matthew J. Franck   "It's Not About Hating Gays," *Pittsburgh Post-Gazette*, December 28, 2010.

Rebecca Hagelin   "Conditioned to Accept a Lie," Townhall.com, September 28, 2010.

Kathryn Jean Lopez   "Being Catholic Means Not Feeling Sorry About Being Catholic," *National Review Online*, June 7, 2010. www.nationalreview.com.

CHAPTER 3

What Methods of Parenthood Should Be Available to Gays and Lesbians?

Chapter Preface

The ability of gay and lesbian couples to adopt a child or to serve as foster parents varies from state to state. To remedy what many supporters of gay-parent adoption see as discrimination, Senator Kirsten Gillibrand of New York and Representative Pete Stark of California introduced Every Child Deserves a Family Act to Congress in 2011. The bill seeks to help children waiting for foster homes or to be adopted by ending state laws that discriminate on the basis of prospective parents' sexual orientation, gender identity, or marital status.

Currently, there are a variety of options available to same-sex couples who want to adopt a child. A joint adoption means that a couple can petition to adopt a child from the biological parent or parents, or a child from the guardianship of the state. As of April 2011, according to the Human Rights Campaign, joint adoption by same-sex couples is permitted in sixteen states—Arkansas, California, Colorado, Connecticut, Illinois, Indiana, Iowa, Maine, Massachusetts, Nevada, New Hampshire, New Jersey, New York, Oregon, Vermont, and Washington—as well as the District of Columbia.

A second-parent adoption allows a person to formally request to adopt his or her partner's child. According to the Human Rights Campaign, as of April 2011, ten states—Arkansas, California, Colorado, Connecticut, Illinois, Massachusetts, New Jersey, New York, Pennsylvania, and Vermont—and Washington, DC, permit second-parent adoptions.

Advances in assisted reproductive technology also have enabled more same-sex couples to become parents, even though the legal ramifications and repercussions are still being mapped out and remain legally murky. Assisted reproductive technology includes in vitro fertilization (IVF), in which sperm and egg are combined in a laboratory dish. A fertilized egg is then transferred to a woman's uterus. One half of a lesbian couple can use her own eggs and either a sperm donor who is known to the couple or an anonymous sperm donor, and then carry the fertilized egg herself. One of the men in a gay couple can donate his own sperm and use a surrogate's eggs; the woman will then carry the child for the couple. While this allows half of a same-sex couple to be the biological parent to a child, it also presents legal consequences for the other parent. As noted above, second-parent adoption is limited across the United States.

According to the Human Rights Campaign, same-sex couples who are considering using a surrogate should consult a lawyer—not only to ensure that there are no issues before IVF is attempted, but also in case of adoption issues after the baby arrives. According to the Human Rights Campaign website, "Subsequently, legal service will be needed to obtain a court order declaring that the intended parents are the sole legal parent(s) and that the surrogate has no parental or legal rights or obligations. The court order will also direct the department of vital records to issue a birth certificate placing the intended parents' name(s) on the certificate."

As more and more same-sex couples become parents—whether as a result of adoption or assisted reproductive technology—the arguments over the impact of gay and lesbian parenthood will continue. The authors of the viewpoints in the following chapter examine the issues that arise when gay men and lesbians adopt, become foster parents, or use assisted reproductive technologies.

> *"Even in couples who choose artificial insemination, in vitro fertilization, or surrogacy, the partner who is not biologically involved must adopt the child."*

Gays and Lesbians Should Be Allowed to Adopt Children

John Ireland

In the following viewpoint, John Ireland claims that many states discriminate against gays and lesbians who want to adopt. He contends that gays and lesbians who want to adopt must become fully aware of their legal rights because of various state laws that prevent the nonbiological parent from being listed on the child's birth certificate. Ireland is a journalist and filmmaker whose short film Finding Family: Gay Adoption in the U.S. *premiered in 2007.*

As you read, consider the following questions:

1. According to Ireland, what is a parent not allowed to do for his or her child if they are not legally related?

2. According to the author, what percentage of children in foster care are not adopted?

John Ireland, "50 Ways to Adopt a Baby," *The Advocate*, August 28, 2007, pp. 39–41. Reproduced by permission.

3. In what does Ireland assert the full faith and credit clause has resulted?

I should mention that I am a filmmaker. At the same time that my partner and I were adopting our foster son, Watson, I began to document stories from social workers, policy makers, and gay and lesbian parents from around the country. My research became a short film called *Finding Family: Gay Adoption in the U.S.* My point was to present the inconsistencies in law and policy across the country that stand in the way of gays and lesbians trying to build our families.

For my documentary I developed a map, labeling states where gay and lesbian couples can and cannot adopt. Perhaps predictably, the eight states that prohibit gay adoption are located in traditionally conservative and rural regions; and the nine states whose laws provide adoption equality for gay and lesbian couples are mostly coastal and metropolitan. But in the vast majority of the country (33 states), gay couples must delicately navigate and manipulate the system.

As an American, I have always felt the bounty of our freedom and liberty. But looking at the map, I see an overwhelming percentage of space where secrecy, ambivalence, and even animus toward our families prevent us from protecting our loved ones. I could not move to a state that does not allow me to protect my son. And so my country has become much smaller.

The entire process gave me invaluable information about the intricacies of gay adoption across the United States. What follows is a look at what I learned—part primer, part travelogue.

Adoption Is Necessary to Secure Parental Rights

Most gay families are touched by adoption. In order to establish a legal relationship to a child who's not biologically related, adoption is necessary. So even in couples who choose artificial insemination, in vitro fertilization, or surrogacy, the partner who is not biologically involved must adopt the child. Without this legal status, he or she is unable to make medical decisions, sign school permission slips, and in some cases, provide health insurance. And in the case of death, he or she may not be able to protect inheritances and select guardians.

Since family law in the U.S. retains language based on the nuclear heterosexual family unit, birth certificates issued by most states list "mother" and "father." And many states refuse to recognize anything different.

Lesson learned: Gay and lesbian parents must seek out competent legal counsel to assure that they are both listed on the birth certificate and both have established parental rights.

Though it is impossible to fully determine its impact, the closet may in fact be helping us in the fight for gay adoption.

As I interviewed families throughout the 33 "ambiguous" states, I encountered a resistance to talking openly about fostering and adopting. One state leader who supports marriage equality suggested that if it became known in his state that gays are adopting children, legislation halting the practice would be "just around the corner." He then added, "It's better we just stay under the radar on this issue here."

Lesson learned: In rural and conservative areas, the adoption closet can be a beneficial, though unfortunate, tool.

Many Countries Will Not Allow Gays and Lesbians to Adopt

Of the 60 or so countries that actively place children in adoptive American families, none will consider applications by gay or lesbian people. Some, like China, Russia, Guatemala, and Vietnam, specifically ask about sexual orientation and will reject gay or lesbian applicants.

Lesson learned: Gays and lesbians can apply as presumably heterosexual singles and then pursue second-parent adoption domestically once the country of origin has completed its

Support for Adoption by Gays and Lesbians Is Growing

A recent *Newsweek* poll [in December 2008] found that support for the adoption rights of homosexuals is up 8 percentage points (45 percent to 53 percent) from 2004, and when it came to the question of rights for nonbiological gay or lesbian parents who've divorced, 63 percent of our respondents said that the partner who is not blood related should still have custody rights and a decision-making role in the child's life.

Lorraine Ali, *"Mrs. Kramer vs. Mrs. Kramer,"*
Newsweek, *December 5, 2008.*

process. The ironic exception to this would be married Massachusetts couples, says Joan Clark, executive director of Adoption Community of New England: "Once they're legally married, they can't sign a document saying they are single. So that, in essence, has closed international adoptions for most gay and lesbian families."

Children in Foster Care Are Suffering

Each year an estimated 120,000 children in foster care are eligible for adoption. Due to a severe shortage of families, nearly 20% will not be placed. Let's make no mistake here; once a child is 2 years old, his chances of being adopted drop significantly. The children who are not matched up with eligible parents become wards of the state, "aging out" into a world where they have no family. It's a devastating prospect.

Lesson learned: Adoption equality for gays and lesbians is essential to adoption reform. John Levesque, a board member for the North American Council on Adoptable Children, believes that "active, honest public recruitment of the gay and lesbian population" would eliminate children lingering in foster care.

Adoption Is Important Because Laws Vary State by State

Family law is the purview of the states, and one state cannot control how other states will view its legal documents. For instance, when a lesbian gives birth to a baby in California, her registered domestic partner is automatically a legal parent and can be named as the second parent on the birth certificate. However, Florida is not likely to give equal consideration to both parents in the case of a separation or divorce, joint custody, and asset division.

Just as states are not required to recognize out-of-state marriage licenses issued to same-sex partners, they periodically refuse to honor out-of-jurisdiction records like birth certificates. However, the full faith and credit clause of the U.S. Constitution [that acknowledges that judicial decisions of one state are recognized by other states] has resulted in courts recognizing other states' judicial judgments, such as an adoption decree.

Lesson learned: Even if gay parents live in a progressive state, attorneys recommend the domestic partner also legally adopt the child. But in every state, it's critical to seek out legal advice to learn what protections partners are afforded.

Of course, all of this effort will be rendered unnecessary when gays and lesbians achieve marriage equality on a nationwide basis. More important, children will not be at the mercy of inconsistent, missing, or defective paperwork. Uniform access to family courts will allow judges to rule in the child's best interest and give legal standing to both parents, and a child will benefit from all the care and support that each parent can give.

Two Dads Adopt Their Foster Children

After successfully foster-parenting 18 needy children over the past few years, Knoxville, Tenn., residents Scott Amos and Tony Frost have many fans in children's services. Nevertheless, in October 2004, Judge Carey Garrett ruled their home "immoral" and ordered the county to remove five foster children.

Social workers rallied to Amos and Frost's defense but were unable to return the children, who subsequently were cycled through other foster homes. Like many of their former foster children, "the kids call us during the holidays and on birthdays," says Amos. "We miss them, and we'll always be here if they need us."

In 2005 a friend of theirs decided to place her newborn child up for adoption and chose Amos and Frost as the parents. Tyler was born on February 23 [2005], and his adoption was finalized on September 6. In November their foster agency placed siblings Dominique and Aaliyah with the couple. Frost says the county social worker initially opposed the placement. "She even spoke with Tyler's mother to convince her that two gay men should not raise her child," he says.

However, over the course of almost a year, the social worker had a change of heart. She came to know Amos and Frost and saw their children flourishing. "Now she's our biggest advocate," Amos explains. "When our foster kids' parents learn that we're two gay men, they march into the office and make a big stink, assuming the worst. But our social workers have built a wall around us, and they go to bat for us."

On August 30, 2006, Amos and Frost celebrated the finalization of Dominique's and Aaliyah's adoptions. And they were joined at the courthouse by a supportive and excited social worker.

> "If the state will not allow the Church to be Church, then, whatever else it does, the Church cannot allow itself to become a social service agency that stinks of incense and good intentions."

Gays and Lesbians Should Not Be Allowed to Adopt Children

Gregory K. Popcak

In the following viewpoint, Gregory K. Popcak contends that gays and lesbians should not be allowed to adopt children despite orders by local governments that adoption agencies allow them to do so or face prosecution for discrimination. He maintains that homosexuality runs contrary to the Catholic Church's teaching that a family must include a mother and father. Popcak is the executive director of the Pastoral Solutions Institute; an author; and the former host of Heart Mind and Strength, *a nationally syndicated radio program.*

As you read, consider the following questions:

1. According to Popcak, why should the Church's work be considered social justice and not social work?

Gregory K. Popcak, "Misplacing Children," *First Things*, vol. 164, June/July 2006, pp. 12–13. Copyright © Institute of Religion and PublicLife June/July 2006. Reproduced by permission.

2. According to the author, what did the American Psychiatric Association decide about homosexuality?

3. By Popcak's estimate, why should there be more than enough heterosexual couples who are willing to adopt?

Attempting social engineering at gunpoint, the state of Massachusetts recently ordered the Catholic Church to place adoptive children with gay and lesbian couples. In response, Catholic Charities of Boston was forced to discontinue its entire adoption program or risk prosecution for its "discriminatory" practices. Although Massachusetts' governor Mitt Romney advocates a bill that would grant religious exemption, the bill is controversial and its passage unlikely. In the wake of these events, other dioceses across the country, such as the archdiocese of San Francisco, have discontinued their practice of placing children with gay and lesbian couples, while still other dioceses, such as the archdiocese of Denver, have reasserted their long-standing policy against the practice.

With a few exceptions, the response from the mainstream media has been the claim that, once again, the Church is allowing strict adherence to its antiquated ideals to interfere with the welfare of flesh-and-blood human beings—and this time, children are obliged to suffer for the Church's folly.

The argument packs a strong emotional punch. On a visceral level, even those who argue that the real issue is religious liberty and not discrimination could understandably feel a profound sadness that an orphaned child's dreams of a home may be delayed or denied for any reason. The best orphanage is still a terrible place for children, and foster care is no replacement for a stable home. Considering the alternatives, there is a strong temptation to seek out any home that will accept the child.

And yet, in "Deus Caritas Est," Pope Benedict asserts that there is a difference between social work and social justice. Mother Teresa observed this when she argued that her Missionaries of Charity "weren't social workers." Social work is about meeting a need, while social justice has to be about meeting the need in a way that chiefly highlights the godly dignity of both the person being served and the person doing the serving. Even if you aren't particular about how your need is met, I undermine the dignity of my own personhood if I serve you in a way that I believe is contrary to your dignity as a child of God. As Pope Benedict wrote, "Those who work for the Church's charitable organizations must be distinguished by the fact that they do not merely meet the needs of the moment, but they dedicate themselves to others with heartfelt concern, enabling them to experience the richness of their humanity. Consequently, in addition to their necessary professional training, these charity workers need a 'formation of the heart': They need to be led to that encounter with God in Christ which awakens their love and opens their spirits to others."

It is tempting to ask what it would hurt. Why shouldn't we let a well-meaning homosexual couple take in a child? But this is the wrong question. The real question is "How can the Church serve at all if the Church is compelled by the state to serve in a manner that detracts from its primary mission—to point to eternal truths, to be a means of sanctification, and to stand as a witness to the Christian anthropological foundations of the human person?" If the state will not allow the Church to be Church, then, whatever else it does, the Church cannot allow itself to become a social service agency that stinks of incense and good intentions.

There is a second objection voiced by those who oppose the Church's stance on placing children with heterosexual couples exclusively. This objection is based on the erroneous belief that the Church's stance is rooted in a fear that children raised by homosexuals will be "turned gay." While the etiology of homosexual attraction continues to be hotly debated, the Church has never said that this is the concern. The 2003 document "Considerations Regarding Proposals to Give Legal Recognition to Unions Between Homosexual Persons," for example, states, "As experience has shown, the absence of sexual complementarity in [homosexual] unions creates obstacles in the normal development of children who would be placed in the care of such persons. They would be deprived of the experience of either fatherhood or motherhood."

Moreover, it is disingenuous to attempt to undermine Church teaching on the natural family by arguing that there is no evidence that children raised by homosexual parents are damaged by the experience: There is no evidence of harm because there is no evidence at all. In their recent book *Destructive Trends in Mental Health: The Well-Intentioned Path to Harm*, Nicholas Cummings and Rogers Wright argue that, especially in the area of sexuality, psychologists have abandoned all pretense of scientific inquiry and allowed themselves to become high priests of a religion of political correctness.

It is well known, for instance, that the American Psychiatric Association declassified homosexuality as a mental disorder by fiat in late 1973. What is less known is that the same resolution insisted on further scientific research and rigorous study of the matter. What is even less known is that, according to Wright and Cummings, no further significant research has been conducted on the matter, much less published in a mainstream, professional, peer-reviewed journal. While other authors have made similar criticisms of the mental health professions, Wright and Cummings' assertions are especially stinging because, in addition to having no cultural agenda to push, they are the two men most responsible for establishing psychology as a medical profession on par with psychiatry and convincing insurers to offer third-party payment for psychotherapy.

Still, wouldn't it be better for the children to give them at least some kind of home? In the event, this question requires

Gay Parents May Pose a Threat to Children

It is important to recognize ... that the highest good, or the child's best interest, is not necessarily *having parents, but having well-being itself.* The two do not necessarily amount to the same thing. We would be loathe, for example, to grant a child to a known pedophile simply for the sake of supplying a parent figure.... To put it another way: Adoption does not solve all ills. There are cases in which the lesser of two evils is for the child to have no parent. There exists the very real possibility that gay parenthood may in fact add to, and not detract from, the angst of the orphan.

Gregory Rogers, *"Suffer the Children: What's Wrong with Gay Adoption?,"* Christian Research Journal, *vol. 28, no. 2, 2005.*

that there are significantly more children waiting to be adopted than there are heterosexual couples waiting to adopt. And this is simply not the case. According to statistics provided by both the National Survey of Family Growth and the Evan B. Donaldson Adoption Institute, there are approximately 120,000 children in the United States waiting to be adopted each year. About half of these are adopted by family members, leaving about 60,000 children who are waiting to be adopted by non-related adoptive parents. By contrast, each year there are anywhere between 70,000 and 162,000 married couples in the United States who have either filed for adoption or are in the process of filing. That means that in any given year there are between 1.2 and 2.7 married couples per waiting child. In other words, there is no child-centered need to open up adoption to homosexual couples.

More, in the unlikely event that there was a state in which there were not enough married, heterosexual couples waiting to adopt, before a Church agency could approve a homosexual adoption it would have to be shown that there were no other regional agencies capable of placing the child. Again, this is not the case. As with most cities, Boston has many adoption agencies, and many of them are more than happy to place children with homosexual couples. There is absolutely no need—unless one allows for the obsessive need of the gay rights movement for cultural validation—to insist that Church agencies change their placement practices.

Even if there were not enough adoptive, married heterosexual couples and there were not a plethora of other agencies offering adoption services, the Church would need to have extraordinarily serious reasons for even considering placing a child with a homosexual couple, especially in the present atmosphere. The absence of a religious-exemption clause in the Massachusetts legislation clearly shows that the sole purpose of this recent initiative was to find some way, any way, to force the Church to accept the legitimacy of gay marriage. If you add to the mix the fact that the diocese in Massachusetts—weakened by its practically criminal response to the sex-abuse scandals—still continues to oppose gay marriage, then you see that the Church of Boston presented a tempting target.

In this politically electrified environment, for the Church to make an individual exception would be tantamount to capitulation to those committed to destroying the natural family. Under less hostile circumstances it might be possible to advance some kind of reasonable casuistry on a very limited basis, perhaps even along the lines as was being practiced before the state attempted to strong-arm the Church. But things being the way they are, it is difficult to imagine how anyone could think that such a pastoral practice would be anything other than material cooperation in the war against the natural family and Christian anthropology.

Despite an understandable tug on the heartstrings, there is simply no substance to any argument against the Church's courageous and ultimately compassionate insistence that all children, especially adoptive children, deserve a mother and a father.

"There's little confusion about what kind of family the Church believes children should have. . . . But I hear too little from the Church about the scandal of one child with no parents."

Gays and Lesbians Should Be Allowed to Be Foster Parents

Todd Flowerday

In the following viewpoint, Todd Flowerday argues that the Catholic Church is being shortsighted when it refuses to allow gays and lesbians to adopt children who need homes. He maintains that the Church focuses too much on the types of parents that it feels each child should have and not enough on the number of children who need homes. Flowerday is the director of liturgy and music for St. Thomas Aquinas Church and Catholic Student Center in Iowa.

As you read, consider the following questions:

1. According to Flowerday, what is AdoptUSKids' purpose?

2. In the author's view, what does he see as the Church's reason for encouraging adoption?

Todd Flowerday, "Children First: How the Church Should Advocate Adoption," *Commonweal*, vol. 136, no. 20, November 20, 2009, pp. 8–9. Copyright © Commonweal Foundation, November 20, 2009. Reproduced by permission of Commonweal Foundation.

3. According to Flowerday, what kind of programs should parishes form to encourage adoption?

November is Adoption Awareness Month in the United States—a national effort to promote the cause of the more than 125,000 children currently in foster care and awaiting adoption. Historically the Catholic Church has invested a great deal of its charitable efforts in the care of orphaned children, but recently adoption has become a battleground for concerns about religious freedom. The Church is reluctant to place children with parents it deems inadequate—most prominently gay and lesbian couples—and these policies often run afoul of state antidiscrimination laws. Rather than compromise, some Catholic agencies get out of the adoption business altogether, as the archdiocese of Boston did in 2006. My own Midwestern diocese will soon follow suit.

It's unfortunate that the Church is abandoning its adoption outreach in these places—and equally unfortunate that an exemption can't be made to allow Catholic Charities to continue to do its work. For Catholics, adoption is more than a useful public program; it is a response to the gospel imperative to serve the poor and powerless. But as an adoptive parent, I am frustrated with the official pronouncements from the Church on the subject of adoption. When the topic is raised, it is often in the service of a political agenda, and usually with a focus on the needs of adults. There's little confusion about what kind of family the Church believes children should have: two parents, a mother and a father, married, stable, and faithful. But I hear too little from the Church about the scandal of one child with no parents.

There are well over a half million children living without parents in the United States today. Many have been separated from their parents for reasons of personal safety. The stated goal of the foster care system is to reunite these young people with their birth families. But there are more than 125,000 children in foster care and institutional homes awaiting adoption, according to a 2006 report from the Adoption and Foster Care Analysis and Reporting System. Most of these children are between the ages of one and fifteen.

The Church no longer runs as many orphanages as it did a century ago. Many dioceses cooperate with outside agencies, sharing information on available children and couples through social workers, in order to place children—most often infants—in adoptive homes. Some work with AdoptUSKids, an initiative of the Department of Health and Human Services that primarily addresses the needs of older foster children. But my sources in diocesan agencies around the United States tell me they do much less work in facilitating adoption than was done in the past. Crisis-pregnancy counseling is still a priority for Catholic Charities, but one diocesan director told me more of their contacts are choosing to keep the baby. In my home diocese, for example, there have been only five placements in the past seven years. This decline is part of the reason my diocese plans to discontinue adoption services, although I was assured that women in crisis pregnancies will be referred to a neighboring diocese or to a private agency.

Catholics often hear about adoption as an alternative in situations when a birth mother is unable or unwilling to care for a baby, and in particular for pregnant women who might be considering an abortion. Adoption also gives childless couples an alternative to fertility treatments that the Church considers immoral. Pope John Paul II mentioned adoption in this context in "Familiaris Consortio" (1981): "It must not be forgotten however that, even when procreation is not possible, conjugal life does not for this reason lose its value. Physical sterility in fact can be for spouses the occasion for other important services to the life of the human person, for example, adoption, various forms of educational work, and assistance to other families and to poor or handicapped children."

It's important to acknowledge the anguish of couples who are unable to conceive—my wife and I were in that boat. The

Church is right to invite infertile couples to live their vocation in other ways. But to me it seems a mark of a certain narcissism that adoption tends to be promoted mainly as a solution for childlessness, rather than as a solution for the child. I see very little encouragement for families with children to consider adoption, despite the tens of thousands of children in foster care who might benefit from joining a stable family. This is a significant blind spot in the Church's moral witness. Our opportunity—and duty—to support life does not end when a child is born. The needs of parentless children ought to be a central concern for every Christian. After all, while it is possible for a marriage to thrive without children, it is much more difficult for children to thrive without parents.

The needs of children are very much a priority for the social workers and state agencies that serve them. My wife and I learned this when we adopted a "special needs" child in 2001, after a search that took years. (The meaning of "special needs" can vary from state to state, and even from one social worker to another; in our daughter's case it means she has a serious medical condition that requires close attention.) We had looked into adopting through Catholic Charities, but my wife had just turned forty—the age limit set by the diocese. We turned instead to the state of Iowa. A social worker we met early in the process told us that her role was to advocate for the kids in her care, with an emphasis on their specific needs. We would have to be our own advocates, she informed us— the social worker's job is to place children well, and that might mean we would be passed over many times as the agency worked to pair children with the parents who were judged best able to care for them. In the end, we were told "no" nearly twenty times before we were finally matched with our then four-year-old daughter.

Many dioceses have curtailed their adoption services in response to laws that would require them to help gay couples adopt. These dioceses seem satisfied to focus their charitable outreach in other areas. I'm not convinced this is a wise course of action. At worst, it looks like petulance. At best, it reveals a lack of imagination when it comes to advocating on behalf of parentless children. My suggestion would be to retool adoption services rather than abandon them outright. The Church could promote a broad, nationwide effort to encourage Catholic married couples (with and without children) to consider adopting children in foster care. Parishes could form adoption awareness-raising and support groups. Social workers could be invited to explain the adoption process, and couples who have been through the process could share their experiences with others. Once the word got out that my wife and I were adopting, we were astonished to discover that many of our friends and acquaintances had already adopted—or had been adopted themselves. Now that we have seen the needs of parentless children, we are eager to spread the word. And what better witness to life could we Catholics give than to help some of those 125,000 girls and boys in foster care?

Adoption is the mutual building of a family, as the judge who presided over our adoption reminded us: My wife and I adopted our daughter; she adopted us. It's a beautiful, complex illustration of what the Church's vision of family can mean, and it's a vital service to the most vulnerable among us. The Church can work harder to call attention to the needs of parentless kids and to encourage more prospective parents to consider this form of self-giving love.

> "*Redefining marriage has a multiplier effect. . . . The problems that we see under mere sexual orientation antidiscrimination laws multiply by order of magnitude when marriage is redefined.*"

Religious Discrimination Occurs When Gays Are Allowed to Be Foster Parents

Dennis Sadowski

In the following viewpoint, Dennis Sadowski argues that the Catholic Church has no choice but to stop running foster care and adoption programs when gay rights are advanced as a civil right. He contends that compelling Church-sponsored programs to place children with gays and lesbians means that the Church is being coerced into accepting homosexuality, which it considers to be immoral. Sadowski is a writer and associate international editor at the Catholic News Service.

As you read, consider the following questions:

1. Why is the diocese of Peoria, IL, no longer taking social service contracts from the state of Illinois, as Sadowski reports?

2. According to the author, why did the Justice Department stop defending the Defense of Marriage Act?

3. In which states have same-sex marriages been legalized, according to Sadowski?

The widening campaign by gay rights advocates to promote same-sex marriage as a civil rights issue is forcing Catholic and other religious institutions to confront charges of intolerance and discrimination.

Also at risk, say Church officials working on the legal front, is the way religious institutions and individuals opposed to same-sex marriage conduct business from hall rentals to receiving government contracts for social services.

Recently, the diocese of Peoria, Ill., withdrew from all state-funded social service contracts, citing increasing clashes between state law and Church teaching on same-sex relationships. The diocese of Rockford stopped offering state-funded adoptions and foster care services when the Illinois civil unions legislation took effect June 1 [2011]. Catholic Charities in the dioceses of Joliet and Springfield and Catholic Social Services of Southern Illinois in Belleville also have been involved in legal proceedings with the state since then.

In 2006, Catholic Charities in San Francisco and Boston stopped adoption placements when laws required equal treatment of applicants in same-sex relationships.

Redefining Marriage Affects Every Aspect of Society

Elsewhere, including New York where a same-sex marriage law took effect July 24, Church institutions are carefully monitoring how such laws are being applied and are vigilant for threats to religious liberty in the areas of taxes, housing, education and employment.

"The general issue is the definition of marriage creates many, many rights, not just one," explained Anthony R. Picarello Jr., general counsel for the U.S. Conference of Catholic Bishops. "So changing the definition of marriage creates changes throughout the legal system."

Those changes can affect a wide range of practices far beyond marriage, such as whether:

- A private individual can deny renting an apartment to a same-sex couple on religious grounds.

- A public school teacher who refuses to talk about same-sex marriage as a justice issue can continue to teach.

- A counselor's license can be revoked for declining to accept same-sex couples as clients.

- A religious organization that does not recognize same-sex marriage can be considered discriminatory by a state or local government and lose any contract for services.

"Redefining marriage has a multiplier effect," Picarello explained to Catholic News Service [CNS]. "The problems proliferate. The problems that we see under mere sexual orientation antidiscrimination laws multiply by order of magnitude when marriage is redefined.

"Marriage is a legal lever, because in our society we have a legal infrastructure that rewards those who support marriage, and punishes those who oppose it. When that legal structure . . . is then applied to a relationship that isn't marriage, the people who object to that definition are going to suffer severe disadvantages," he added.

Picarello pointed to the February announcement by the Justice Department that it would no longer defend the Defense of Marriage Act—DOMA—because it is biased and prejudicial against homosexuals and therefore is discriminatory among the mounting challenges facing religious institutions opposed to same-sex marriage.

The Church Is Unfairly Portrayed as Being Bigoted

"They basically suggested that any law that distinguishes between same-sex couples and different-sex couples, whether it's for purposes of marriage or anything else, violates the Constitution if the government is doing it, (that) the government can't make those distinctions," Picarello said.

"But all DOMA does is define marriage as it's always been defined," he said. "The Church stands behind that definition and now the Church has been lumped in with bigots and haters."

For states to imply such a comparison is a major leap because it dismisses religious tradition and the morality of same-sex relationships while portraying religious objections to same-sex marriage as equivalent to racial discrimination.

The religious liberty issue has largely been played out at the state level. Same-sex marriage has been legalized through legislation or by court decisions in Connecticut, Iowa, Massachusetts, New Hampshire, New York, Vermont and the District of Columbia. Illinois and Rhode Island this year enacted civil union laws; come Jan. 1 [2012] civil unions will become legal in Delaware and Hawaii.

In California, Proposition 8, a ballot initiative approved by voters in 2008 to ban same-sex marriage, remains in the courts and may end up at the U.S. Supreme Court.

Same-sex marriage is banned by law or constitutional amendment in the remaining 40 states.

Some States Have Allowed Religious Exemptions

In states where same-sex marriage has been enacted by law, at least a basic religious exemption has been included. The breadth of the exemption varies with some jurisdictions offering a general exemption from performing same-sex marriages to more wide-ranging protections like those in Connecticut that spell out specific protections for religious institutions.

Michael C. Culhane, executive director of the Connecticut Catholic [Public Affairs] Conference, lobbied for three exemptions following the state Supreme Court's 2008 decision that legalized same-sex marriage.

In addition to the normal exemption for clergy from participating in a same-sex marriage ceremony, Connecticut's law has one provision protecting fraternal societies from providing insurance benefits to anyone if doing so violates the free exercise of religion and another safeguarding the rights of a religious organization in the delivery of adoption, foster care or social services as long as government funds are not involved.

"In the long hours we ended up with a very strong religious exemption," Culhane said. "We were very, very happy."

In Iowa, where the state Supreme Court ruled that same-sex marriage is legal, Tom Chapman, executive director of the Iowa Catholic Conference, said the Church has been minimally affected by the court's decision.

"We have the same concerns a lot of places do and would have," he said. "For example, Catholic schools in Iowa are accredited by the state. So anything that can be required in public schools can be required in Catholic schools as well."

The likelihood that the issue will be addressed by the legislature is slim, Chapman told CNS.

"My own feeling is there is a desire on everybody's part who wants same-sex marriage to leave it alone because they don't want us to have a defense of marriage amendment or legislation (that could restrict same-sex marriage)," he said.

The Government Is Ordering the Church to Go Against Its Teachings

Such an exemption in Illinois civil unions law failed to resolve the dilemma faced by the Peoria diocese. The predicament arose when state Department of Children and Family Services mandated that the diocesan Catholic Charities system end the practice of referring adoptions and foster placements to same-sex couples to another agency. Catholic Charities appealed, but lost in court, leading the diocese to back out of all state contracts for social services.

Robert Gilligan, executive director of the Catholic Conference of Illinois, told CNS that state law affords protections for religious practice, but that the state has the right to contract with any agency for the delivery of services.

"The danger is that faith-based organizations will get crowded out of the provision of services that are desperately needed," he said.

Even with specific exemptions for religious institutions, individuals everywhere face possible infringements on the practice of their faith, said Daniel Avila, policy adviser for marriage and family to the U.S. bishops' Subcommittee for the Promotion and Defense of Marriage.

"Even if you think you're protected and this is not an issue in your own state, given you have a state DOMA, they should be quite aware of events happening at the national level that could then bring these very issues and problems into their own lives," he said.

Avila suggested that at least two cases, including California's legal battle over Proposition 8, will likely make their way to the U.S. Supreme Court and determine the legal status of same-sex marriage in the country.

The cases are likely two years away, he said.

That leaves states to follow their own course on what actions are discriminatory and what are not, and religious organizations guessing which way they will go.

> "The importance of genetics when it comes to parenting, or to the child's own psychological and emotional growth, is downplayed, if not ignored."

The Genetic Ties of Assisted Reproduction Must Be Considered

Liza Mundy

In the following viewpoint, Liza Mundy contends that while assisted reproduction has allowed the conception of children who do not necessarily share a genetic history with their parents, it also has created a dynamic in which the significance of knowing one's genetic history is gradually being disregarded. She argues that there is a vital parent-child bond that comes with shared genes that each child deserves to know. Mundy is the author of Everything Conceivable: How Assisted Reproduction Is Changing Our World, *which was published in 2007.*

As you read, consider the following questions:

1. According to the author, what is "collaborative reproduction"?

2. In Mundy's opinion, how does the phrase "genetics don't matter—except when they do" explain what happened in the "Baby M" case?

3. According to the author, what did a study conducted by the Sperm Bank of California find that most children of anonymous sperm donors want?

There's a lot we don't know about the pregnancy of Mary Cheney [the daughter of former vice president Dick Cheney]—but a few things we do. We know that the vice president's openly gay 37-year-old daughter is expecting a baby whom her parents are happily preparing to welcome as their sixth grandchild. We know that she plans to raise the child with her longtime partner, Heather Poe. And we know that there must be a man involved somewhere—either a friend or acquaintance (a "known donor") or a donor from a sperm bank.

In short, we know that this pregnancy involves what's called, in the fertility business, "collaborative reproduction."

Redefining the Meaning of Family

That's the trade term for a situation in which a couple (or a single person) conceives with help from a third party who probably won't be involved in raising the child, but who agrees, as one egg broker put it, to "genetically contribute to the conception process." It's a situation unprecedented in human history, but now common to the point of being commonplace. Yet these technologies are setting in motion a social experiment that will unfold over decades, creating hundreds of thousands of families in which the role of genetic ties will be newly tested—and the meaning of family reevaluated.

In the United States, donated sperm is used in 80,000 to 100,000 inseminations each year. In 2003, at least 15,000 in vitro fertilization [IVF] procedures—in which the gametes, a woman's eggs and a man's sperm, are united in a petri dish and the resulting embryos are transferred into a uterus—were performed with donated eggs; that number grows by 20 percent annually. More than 1,000 babies are born each year through surrogacy, in which a woman carries a child for another woman or, increasingly, for two gay men.

These explosively popular science-enabled multi-parent arrangements are altering our understanding of what parents are and how families can be formed. And they're confusing our thinking about genetic relationship and its importance to the parent-child bond. Collaborative reproduction is becoming widespread at precisely the moment when we've become ultra-aware of how genes run the show in the unfolding of a human being: controlling everything from physical attributes such as height and hair color to a predisposition for certain illnesses to a tendency toward shyness or a taste for fine wine.

Interviewing hundreds of families for a book on assisted reproduction, I've been struck by how conscious people are of the power of genetic inheritance—and yet how bewildered they are about how a missing genetic connection might affect their family.

Infertility Has Become a Profit-Making Business

Reproductive medicine and the profit-making industry that has grown up around it send a powerfully mixed message, encouraging parents to accept that genes are crucial to the formation of their children, yet irrelevant to the formation of a relationship with those children. Genes matter, the message is, except when they don't.

"Let's face it: Donor gametes is an experiment," one fertility doctor aptly put it. "Who the hell knows how it's going to turn out?"

An irony of assisted reproductive technology is that it was invented to help infertile couples have biological children, yet quickly became a way for people to knowingly conceive children who would be biologically related to just one parent.

Only six years after IVF first succeeded in 1978, with the birth of Louise Brown to a British couple, doctors discovered that it was startlingly easy to achieve a pregnancy in a woman by using eggs from another. By the 1990s, egg donation had caught on as a way to help women in their late 30s and 40s whose eggs were no longer viable. So popular is egg donation in Washington [DC] that one clinic scours rural Pennsylvania for donors. The area's more than 15 clinics compete with ads hyping the quantity and quality of available donors.

Meanwhile, sperm donation has been around for more than a century. The first known procedure was performed in 1884 by a doctor who inseminated an anesthetized patient with sperm from a medical student, without asking her permission or telling her afterward. By World War II, donor sperm was a routine "treatment" offered to married couples. In 1992, a variant of IVF in which a single sperm cell can be injected into an egg made it possible for many infertile men to have biological children. Since then, single women and lesbians have become the majority of the clientele seeking sperm donation.

There Is an Emotional Connection That Comes with Shared Genes

People selecting a donor are bombarded with information about the donor's likely genes. Web sites for sperm banks and egg brokerages invite prospective parents to sort anonymous donors based on ethnicity, College Board scores, personality tests, shade of skin and curl of hair. For a fee, they can order childhood photographs or scrutinize a handwriting sample. "One of them couldn't spell; she spelled 'Catholic' wrong," one mother told me wryly. She rejected that donor.

The message is that genetics are everything—everything—in the formation of your child. And parents of course believe they owe the child the best genes. As one gay couple put it: "What are you going to do—get someone with a 1550 [SAT score], or are you going to cheat your child and get them a mom with a 1210?" In choosing their egg donor, they made a decision tree assigning values to attributes they were looking for.

Yet even as these genetic profiles are being posted and peddled, the importance of genetics when it comes to parenting, or to the child's own psychological and emotional growth, is downplayed, if not ignored. The message here is: Your child won't be related to you, but she will still love you, no problem. Every day, families are being formed by parents trying to hold in their heads the competing notions that genes, while important, aren't. Genetics matter—except when they don't.

Is gamete donation like adoption? "I've always looked at this as adoption that is run by the medical profession," says Bill Cordray, now in his 60s, who is part of a group of donor offspring agitating for the right to know their donors' identities, arguing that people denied that knowledge are unable to understand themselves. Accepting this argument, some countries, such as Britain, have banned anonymous donation.

But in the United States, many egg and sperm brokers disagree. They point out that adoption involves the grief of relinquishing an actual baby. In donation, nobody's relinquishing. Everybody's happy. What a child needs, they say, is not a relationship with the genetic parent, but a coherent narrative about the way he or she was born.

Yet the industry tacitly recognizes that genetic connection can matter. In the late 1980s, a surrogate [Mary Beth Whitehead] in New Jersey contracted to be inseminated and to surrender her own biological offspring to the father and his wife. But after giving birth, she didn't want to give up the child. A court forced her to do so—in the famous "Baby M" case. As a result, most surrogates now are "gestational carriers," bearing babies created with eggs that are not their own. Everyone assumes that having no genetic relationship will make it easier for a surrogate to hand over the baby. Genetics don't matter—except when they do.

Children of Sperm Donors Will Forever Have a Biological Connection to the Donor

Donor offspring may have legal and social parents who take a variety of forms—single, coupled, gay, straight. But they also have, like everyone else, a biological father and mother, two people whose very beings are found in the child's own body and seen in his or her own image reflected in the mirror.

Karen Clark and Elizabeth Marquardt,
"The Sperm-Donor Kids Are Not Really All Right,"
Slate, June 14, 2010. www.slate.com.

In two-parent families, many parents still don't tell children they are donor-conceived. "Parents are afraid that if they tell the child they are not the genetic parent, the child will love them less," Fay Johnson, a longtime surrogacy broker, told me. Though the donor has no legal claim, parents worry that he or she possesses some kind of unarticulated blood claim, and they fear that person's power. "I'm the dad, damn it," I was told by one man, who thought that if his sons grew up and wanted to track down their donor, it would be a sign that he had failed as a father. One mother told me about dreams in which her anonymous egg donor knocked on her door, asked to see her son, and left taking both the son and the woman's husband with her.

More Counseling Is Needed

And of course, children don't always see things the way their parents do. The Sperm Bank of California, a small nonprofit established in 1982 to serve mostly lesbians and single women, has pioneered an "identity release" program that entitles offspring, at 18, to learn the identity of their donors. In a study conducted as the first deadline for tracking down donors approached, the bank found that though most children were comfortable with their origins and regarded the people who had raised them as their parents, most still wanted to meet their donors. And many more than anticipated wanted a relationship with the donor.

Collaborative reproduction has brought happiness to many, and children to millions. There aren't enough adoptable children in the United States to meet people's desire for kids and family life. And there are men and women who are comfortable giving away an egg or sperm. The result is children who, by and large, will be glad to have been born.

But it's wrong when an industry stokes the genetic anxieties of would-be parents yet fails to provide the support to help us all figure out how to deal with the ways in which genetics do affect family ties. It's also wrong when would-be parents get shuttled along too quickly. Some women now go through IVF one or two times and, if it fails, are encouraged to move on to egg donation as if it's merely another step in a medical process.

Like adoption agencies, clinics need to acknowledge that you can't just slip a new set of genes into the conception process and go on as though nothing had happened. They need to connect parents with counselors who know the research. Egg-donation recipients typically receive an hour's worth of counseling; sperm bank patrons often get none. Yet these families are going to unfold in unexpected directions.

Not long ago, I interviewed a mother who had conceived twin daughters with the help of an egg donor. At a wedding, she ran into the donor, who was a casual acquaintance. The woman did not want children and was glad to help someone who did. But the donor's parents were also at the wedding, and the girls' mother noticed them looking at her twins. They were the girls' genetic grandparents, looking, a little wistfully, at the granddaughters they would never have.

What is a donor? What are a donor's parents? The reproductive field needs to acknowledge that these questions exist, and that the answers matter. After all, the Cheneys won't be the only genetic grandparents of Mary's baby. Presumably, there will be another set out there—somewhere.

> *"We are here to adapt and evolve and try to clue into the Mystery. And playing with reproduction and family structure is one hell of an often glorious, often tortuous way to do exactly that."*

Alternative Reproduction and Family Structures Will Continue to Evolve

Mark Morford

In the following viewpoint, Mark Morford argues that life is constantly evolving and so must the idea of the traditional family structure. He contends that while families with children conceived through surrogacy and sperm donation are not perfect, neither are traditional families. Morford is an opinion columnist and writer for the San Francisco Chronicle.

As you read, consider the following questions:

1. According to Morford, which part of society is offended by the changes in the traditional family structure?

2. In the author's view, what are some of the basic things needed for any family, regardless of how it is formed?

3. According to Morford, what type of issues can complicate matters in egg or sperm donations?

I have a friend who has a very young and beautiful son with a woman to whom he is not married or even dating and with whom he has never actually had sex because he is quite perfectly in love with someone else and she is quite perfectly single and, well, it's sort of out of the question.

My friend, however, is, as they say, good breeding stock. This seems to be the consensus. He is light and luminous and strong and tall and beautiful and his apparent spermal excellence is evidenced by the fact that the mother of their happy beautiful child would very much like to have another child using another dose of the high-quality DNA of my friend. And so would, he tells me, two other women.

It is a proposal he is quite modestly and humbly considering, given that he is openhearted and generous and also because he has been, to his peaceful dismay, requested to act only as casual and hush-hush part-time quasi-parent with his first child. Such is the way.

It is a situation that, as you might imagine, creates all manner of curious parenting dynamics and intriguing emotional conflicts, messy and strange. And my friend is, of course, far from alone.

Nontraditional Families Are Becoming More Common

This is San Francisco. This is what you do. Modern twists on the staid ol' family format are much more accepted and expected in this glorious liberal bubble of progress and experimentation, and few people raise an eyebrow when they hear of happily unusual breeding practices that casually flout traditional pseudo-Christian 50-percent-divorce-rate nuclear family values.

I know unmarried women in their 40s who very much want babies and who have yet to meet the right guy and so have naturally considered the semi-creepy world of sperm banks or asking friends or maybe posting something unusual on Craigslist. I know kinky polyamorous [having more than one intimate relationship] couples who are working toward babydom, on their own terms, multiple relationships intact. I know of lesbian couples who've adopted boy babies and gay male couples who've adopted girl babies and straight couples who've adopted baffled toddlers from China.

I know of all types of couples—gay, straight and in between—who've brought in surrogate mothers or sperm-donating friends and swapped eggs and semen and vials and tubes and syringes and fertilization tips and laughter and cocktails, and it's all good and happy and progressive until someone loses a zygote [a developing individual formed through the union of an egg and sperm].

Such giddy rearrangements of the traditional family pieces is a terrific and good thing, overall, despite (or perhaps exactly because of) how much consternation and pain such recon-figuration induces in the vicious religious right. Because the fact is, by almost any measure, the traditional, man-woman, Christian family configuration has been an abject failure, an utter embarrassment to time and culture and the art of favor-able statistics. Oh yes it has.

Show me a single scientific experiment where fully 50 per-cent of the results turn out negative and induce collapse and emotional breakdown and childhood therapy and Xanax and alcoholism and screaming, and I'll show you a scientist who will quickly scrap the whole thing and start all over. Which is not to say it's not one hell of a lot of wicked fun to try any-way, should you be wired that way. You just gotta know your odds.

No Family Is Perfect

But then it appears the quirky alt-family options aren't exactly gilded slabs of congenial bliss, either. Seems a funny thing

My Daughters Benefit from Having Two Moms and a Dad

The real gift is the one I received: a family with a pair of little girls who are profoundly fortunate to have two devoted, strong, courageous moms. My daughters have three loving parents and live with two of them.

Mike Livingston, "My Life as a Sperm Donor Dad,"
Washington Post, *December 17, 2006.*

happened on the way to the alternative family: People still have issues. People still have just a tremendous number of hang-ups and emotional dramas regarding family and babies and who the hell gets to shape and mold and influence the consciousness of another human life. Go figure.

This is what we're learning: It does not matter if you're Christian or gay or bi, Mormon or neocon or a rainbow-colored leather-clad bear with hair where your legs used to be. Issues arise. Emotions tumble forth. There is, apparently, no perfect way. There is no ideal family structure, and quit pointing to your Bible before you hurt yourself—Rule No. 1 in all matters reproductive: Never trust musty dogmatic mythology written by angry old men who never had sex. Duh.

We do know one thing. There are only a few key ingredients that work every single time. They are: stability, deep love, laughter, honest communication, solid boundaries, human kindness, balance and chocolate ice cream. That's about it. There is only the impulse to love and connect and carry on. And maybe, now and then, a good hot bath.

For a while, my friend was troubled by the fact that he was supposed to be close with his child and help take care of him and celebrate their love, and yet he has been instructed not to tell anyone he's the father because, well, the mother had issues (they later revised this plan after realizing that hiding such significant details from this child would only screw him up and induce resentment and possibly turn him Republican, so they invented a bedtime story telling of his charmed birth and his loving community and how they all lived happily ever after).

Then again, a wonderful lesbian couple I know used the sperm of a gay friend to become pregnant and have given birth, only to suffer a major falling-out with the donor, and now he wants access to the kid, which violates the spirit of their agreement, and hence he and the couple hate each other and no one's the slightest bit happy.

It can get convoluted. Sperm-bank kids may never know that a thing like a father exists or that Mom was just too, um, "unique" to find a mate. Spouses of egg or sperm donors can become crazy-jealous that their lover shared such intimate genetics with another, and hence marriages get ruined and relationships get tangled and none of this even touches on what happens when the kid comes of age and wants to know what the hell is going on—and by the way, where's Dad?

The Definition of a Family Must Evolve

For every success story in the alternative-family sphere, there's a debilitating wrinkle. It is perhaps no better—or worse— than traditional structures. But for every major falling-out and nasty emotional entanglement, there's a mad success story resulting in a glorious kid (or three) who will be raised with a funky and fresh perspective on family and parenting which, oh my God, we so desperately need in this culture right now that we might as well be in a desert pleading for water.

It would seem there is no escaping the human drama. It would seem there is no way around personal issues of life and sperm and DNA and pulse. You may thump your revisionist Bible, you may cite your lopsided studies, you may wave your freak flags high, but the truth is we are here on this planet to work toward the new. We are here to adapt and evolve and try to clue into the Mystery. And playing with reproduction and family structure is one hell of an often glorious, often tortuous way to do exactly that. What, you thought we were all done? Not even close.

Periodical and Internet Sources Bibliography

The following articles have been selected to supplement the diverse views presented in this chapter.

Ronald Bailey	"Who's Your Daddy? Or Your Other Daddy? Or Your Mommy?," *Reason*, January 5, 2010.
Steve Chapman	"Gay Adoption: The Real Agenda," Townhall.com, November 30, 2008.
Maggie Gallagher	"Banned in Boston," *Weekly Standard*, May 15, 2006.
Cal Greene	"Door Conception and Children's Rights: A Parent's Decision," *Canadian Medical Association Journal*, February 22, 2011.
Dahlia Lithwick	"Why Courts Are Adopting Gay Parenting," *Washington Post*, March 12, 2006.
Elizabeth Marquardt	"'My Daddy's Name Is Donor,'" *Chicago Tribune*, May 15, 2005.
Thomas Messner	"Another Christian Adoption Agency Burdened by State-Sponsored Intolerance," *The Foundry*, May 23, 2011. http://blog.heritage.org.
Pamela Paul	"The Battle Over a Baby," *New York Times Magazine*, July 22, 2009.
Roger Scruton	"This 'Right' for Gays Is an Injustice to Children," *Telegraph* (UK), January 28, 2007.
Margaret Somerville	"Life's Essence, Bought and Sold," *Globe and Mail* (Canada), July 9, 2010.
Peter Sprigg	"Good News About Adoptive Parents—But Not About Same-Sex Couples," *Human Events*, March 13, 2007.

OPPOSING
VIEWPOINTS®
SERIES

What Laws Should Regulate Gay Parenting?

Chapter Preface

As the debate continues over what effect families headed by gay, lesbian, bisexual, and transgender couples have on society, the legal battles over whether society should recognize them grow as well.

Washington State became the latest state to legalize same-sex marriages when Democratic governor Christine Gregoire signed legislation on February 13, 2012, allowing gay men and lesbians to marry there. Opponents are already working to put a referendum on the November 2012 ballot that would repeal the law. Joseph Backholm, executive director of the Family Policy Institute of Washington, echoes the beliefs of many who oppose gay marriage because of the belief that society's very fabric is stretched to the breaking point with anything that legitimizes gay and lesbian families. A February 13, 2012, press release from the institute reflects this view: "Marriage is society's way of bringing men and women together so that children can be raised by, and cared for by, their mother and father—the people responsible for bringing them into the world. It is the most important child-focused institution of society and we will fight to preserve it. Voters will have the opportunity to define marriage in our state."

Supporters of same-sex marriage argue that gay and lesbian couples should enjoy the same rights as heterosexual couples to begin a life together. On January 4, 2012, before signing the bill, Governor Gregoire said, "When someone asks me what marriage means, I don't think about the legal protections of a marriage license. I think about love, commitment, responsibility and partnership. Same-sex couples should not be denied the meaning of marriage. They have a right to be equal."

Washington follows six other states in recognizing the rights of gays and lesbians to legally marry; the other states are Connecticut, Iowa, Massachusetts, New Hampshire, New York, and Vermont. Same-sex marriage is also legal in the District of Columbia. Same-sex civil unions are allowed in Hawaii, Delaware, Illinois, New Jersey, and Rhode Island, according to the National Conference of State Legislatures.

The legal battles across the country show no sign of abating anytime soon. On February 7, 2012, the Ninth US Circuit Court of Appeals ruled that California's Proposition 8 is unconstitutional. The proposition, which California voters approved in November 2008, banned same-sex marriage in that state. This amendment came about after the California Supreme Court upheld that the California constitution's equal protection clause was being violated by denying same-sex couples the right to marry. Gay and lesbian couples began marrying in California in June 2008. The case went to federal court after Judge Vaughn Walker ruled on August 4, 2010, that the amendment was unconstitutional.

New Jersey's state senate approved a same-sex marriage bill on February 13, 2012, that is expected to pass in the state's assembly as well but is expected to be vetoed by Republican governor Chris Christie. Meanwhile in Maryland, legislators began working in early 2012 on a same-sex marriage bill in that state.

Complicating the debate over same-sex marriages and civil unions is the issue of the rights of gay, lesbian, bisexual, and transgender people, including their right to become parents. The authors of the viewpoints in the following chapter debate the effects of same-sex marriage on traditional marriage, whether same-sex partners and parents deserve the same legal rights as heterosexual couples, and the effects of same-sex marriages on children.

> "The big idea is to stop the erosion of society's most pro-child institution. Gay marriage is only one facet of the larger threat to the institution."

Same-Sex Marriages Weaken Traditional Marriages

David Blankenhorn

In the following viewpoint, David Blankenhorn asserts that allowing gay men and lesbians to marry damages and weakens the traditional concept of marriage. He argues that same-sex marriage also leads to more lax attitudes toward children, sex, and monogamy. Blankenhorn is the president of the Institute for American Values and the author of The Future of Marriage.

As you read, consider the following questions:

1. According to Blankenhorn, how do people in countries with same-sex marriage feel about marriage in general?

2. What are some of the "marriage-weakening attitudes and behaviors" cited by the author?

3. How does Blakenhorn identify "deinstitutionalization"?

David Blankenhorn, "Defining Marriage Down . . . Is No Way to Save It," *The Weekly Standard*, vol. 12, no. 28, April 2, 2007. Copyright © 2010 Weekly Standard LLC. Reproduced by permission.

Does permitting same-sex marriage weaken marriage as a social institution? Or does extending to gay and lesbian couples the right to marry have little or no effect on marriage overall? Scholars and commentators have expended much effort trying in vain to wring proof of causation from the data— all the while ignoring the meaning of some simple correlations that the numbers do indubitably show.

Much of the disagreement among scholars centers on how to interpret trends in the Netherlands and Scandinavia. Stanley Kurtz has argued, in this magazine [*Weekly Standard*] and elsewhere, that the adoption of gay marriage or same-sex civil unions in those countries has significantly weakened customary marriage, already eroded by easy divorce and stigma-free cohabitation.

William Eskridge, a Yale Law School professor, and Darren R. Spedale, an attorney, beg to differ. In *Gay Marriage: For Better or for Worse?*, a book-length reply to Kurtz, they insist that Kurtz does not prove that gay marriage is causing anything in those nations; that Nordic marriage overall appears to be healthier than Kurtz allows; and that even if marriage is declining in that part of the world, "the question remains whether that phenomenon is a lamentable development."

Eskridge and Spedale want it both ways. For them, there is no proof that marriage has weakened, but if there were it wouldn't be a problem. For people who care about marriage, this perspective inspires no confidence. Eskridge and Spedale do score one important point, however. Neither Kurtz nor anyone else can scientifically prove that allowing gay marriage causes the institution of marriage to get weaker. Correlation does not imply causation. The relation between two correlated phenomena may be causal, or it may be random, or it may reflect some deeper cause producing both. Even if you could show that every last person in North Carolina eats barbecue, you would not have established that eating barbecue is a result of taking up residence in North Carolina.

When it comes to the health of marriage as an institution and the legal status of same-sex unions, there is much to be gained from giving up the search for causation and studying some recurring patterns in the data, as I did for my book *The Future of Marriage*. It turns out that certain clusters of beliefs about and attitudes toward marriage consistently correlate with certain institutional arrangements. The correlations crop up in a large number of countries and recur in data drawn from different surveys of opinion.

Take the International Social Survey Programme (ISSP), a collaborative effort of universities in over 40 countries. It interviewed about 50,000 adults in 35 countries in 2002. What is useful for our purposes is that respondents were asked whether they agreed or disagreed with six statements that directly relate to marriage as an institution:

- Married people are generally happier than unmarried people.

- People who want children ought to get married.

- One parent can bring up a child as well as two parents together.

- It is all right for a couple to live together without intending to get married.

- Divorce is usually the best solution when a couple can't seem to work out their marriage problems.

- The main purpose of marriage these days is to have children.

Let's stipulate that for statements one, two, and six, an "agree" answer indicates support for traditional marriage as an authoritative institution. Similarly, for statements three, four, and five, let's stipulate that agreement indicates a lack of support, or less support, for traditional marriage.

Then divide the countries surveyed into four categories: those that permit same-sex marriage; those that permit same-sex civil unions (but not same-sex marriage); those in which some regions permit same-sex marriage; and those that do not legally recognize same-sex unions.

There Is Less Support for Marriage Where There Is Same-Sex Marriage

The correlations are strong. Support for marriage is by far the weakest in countries with same-sex marriage. The countries with marriage-like civil unions show significantly more support for marriage. The two countries with only regional recognition of gay marriage (Australia and the United States) do better still on these support-for-marriage measurements, and those without either gay marriage or marriage-like civil unions do best of all.

In some instances, the differences are quite large. For example, people in nations with gay marriage are less than half as likely as people in nations without gay unions to say that married people are happier. Perhaps most important, they are significantly less likely to say that people who want children ought to get married (38 percent vs. 60 percent). They are also significantly more likely to say that cohabiting without intending to marry is all right (83 percent vs. 50 percent), and are somewhat more likely to say that divorce is usually the best solution to marital problems. Respondents in the countries with gay marriage are significantly more likely than those in Australia and the United States to say that divorce is usually the best solution.

A similar exercise using data from a different survey yields similar results. The World Values Survey, based in Stockholm, Sweden, periodically interviews nationally representative samples of the public of some 80 countries on six continents—over 100,000 people in all—on a range of issues. It contains three statements directly related to marriage as an institution:

1. A child needs a home with both a father and a mother to grow up happily.

2. It is all right for a woman to want a child but not a stable relationship with a man.

3. Marriage is an outdated institution.

Again grouping the countries according to the legal status of same-sex unions, the data from the 1999–2001 wave of interviews yield a clear pattern. Support for marriage as an institution is weakest in those countries with same-sex marriage. Countries with same-sex civil unions show more support, and countries with regional recognition show still more. By significant margins, support for marriage is highest in countries that extend no legal recognition to same-sex unions.

So what of it? Granted that these correlations may or may not reflect causation, what exactly can be said about the fact that certain values and attitudes and legal arrangements tend to cluster?

Here's an analogy. Find some teenagers who smoke, and you can confidently predict that they are more likely to drink than their nonsmoking peers. Why? Because teen smoking and drinking tend to hang together. What's more, teens who engage in either of these activities are also more likely than nonsmokers or nondrinkers to engage in other risky behaviors, such as skipping school, getting insufficient sleep, and forming friendships with peers who get into trouble.

Because these behaviors correlate and tend to reinforce one another, it is virtually impossible for the researcher to pull out any one from the cluster and determine that it alone is causing or is likely to cause some personal or (even harder to measure) social result. All that can be said for sure is that these things go together. To the degree possible, parents hope that their children can avoid all of them, the entire syndrome—drinking, smoking, skipping school, missing sleep,

Traditional Marriages Have Always Been Accepted Universally

Humanity knows many different forms of relationships: close friendships, cousins, aunts and uncles, and nieces and nephews, brothers and sisters. Why is it that every society throughout human history has favored the relationship between a man and a woman who commit to one another? And why is it that this unique relationship is called "marriage," and nothing else is?

For those answers, we can turn to anthropologists. They tell us that natural marriage—a union between a man and a woman—is humanly and historically universal. Never, until the last few milliseconds of human history, has any society had homosexual marriage.

Randy Hicks,
"The Cultural Argument Against Gay Marriage,"
byFaith, *October 2006.*

and making friends with other children who get into trouble—in part because each of them increases exposure to the others.

Same-Sex Marriage and Traditional Marriage Clash

It's the same with marriage. Certain trends in values and attitudes tend to cluster with each other and with certain trends in behavior. A rise in unwed childbearing goes hand in hand with a weakening of the belief that people who want to have children should get married. High divorce rates are encountered where the belief in marital permanence is low. More one-parent homes are found where the belief that children need both a father and a mother is weaker. A rise in nonmarital cohabitation is linked at least partly to the belief that marriage as an institution is outmoded. The legal endorsement of gay marriage occurs where the belief prevails that marriage itself should be redefined as a private personal relationship. And all of these marriage-weakening attitudes and behaviors are linked. Around the world, the surveys show, these things go together.

Eskridge and Spedale are right. We cannot demonstrate statistically what exactly causes what, or what is likely to have what consequences in the future. But we do see in country after country that these phenomena form a pattern that recurs. They are mutually reinforcing. Socially, an advance for any of them is likely to be an advance for all of them. An individual who tends to accept any one or two of them probably accepts the others as well. And as a political and strategic matter, anyone who is fighting for any one of them should—almost certainly already does—support all of them, since a victory for any of them clearly coincides with the advance of the others. Which is why, for example, people who have devoted much of their professional lives to attacking marriage as an institution almost always favor gay marriage. These things do go together.

Inevitably, the pattern discernible in the statistics is borne out in the statements of the activists. Many of those who most vigorously champion same-sex marriage say that they do so precisely in the hope of dethroning once and for all the traditional "conjugal institution."

That phrase comes from Judith Stacey, professor of sociology at New York University [NYU] and a major expert witness testifying in courts and elsewhere for gay marriage. She views the fight for same-sex marriage as the "vanguard site" for rebuilding family forms. The author of journal articles like "Good Riddance to 'The Family' [: A Response to David Popenoe]," she argues forthrightly that "if we begin to value the meaning and quality of intimate bonds over their customary forms, there are few limits to the kinds of marriage and kinship patterns people might wish to devise."

Similarly, David L. Chambers, a law professor at the University of Michigan widely published on family issues, favors gay marriage for itself but also because it would likely "make society receptive to the further evolution of the law." What kind of evolution? He writes, "If the deeply entrenched paradigm we are challenging is the romantically linked man-woman couple, we should respect the similar claims made against the hegemony of the two-person unit and against the romantic foundations of marriage."

Examples could be multiplied—the recently deceased Ellen Willis, professor of journalism at NYU and head of its center for cultural reporting and criticism, expressed the hope that gay marriage would "introduce an implicit revolt against the institution into its very heart, further promoting the democratization and secularization of personal and sexual life"—but they can only illustrate the point already established by the large-scale international comparisons: Empirically speaking, gay marriage goes along with the erosion, not the shoring up, of the institution of marriage.

Gay Marriage Is Part of a Larger Threat to Traditional Marriage

These facts have two implications. First, to the degree that it makes any sense to oppose gay marriage, it makes sense only if one also opposes with equal clarity and intensity the other main trends pushing our society toward post-institutional marriage. After all, the big idea is not to stop gay marriage. The big idea is to stop the erosion of society's most pro-child institution. Gay marriage is only one facet of the larger threat to the institution.

Similarly, it's time to recognize that the beliefs about marriage that correlate with the push for gay marriage do not exist in splendid isolation, unrelated to marriage's overall institutional prospects. Nor do those values have anything to do with strengthening the institution, notwithstanding the much-publicized but undocumented claims to the contrary from those making the "conservative case" for gay marriage.

Instead, the deep logic of same-sex marriage is clearly consistent with what scholars call deinstitutionalization—the overturning or weakening of all of the customary forms of marriage, and the dramatic shrinking of marriage's public meaning and institutional authority. Does deinstitutionalization necessarily require gay marriage? Apparently not. For decades heterosexuals have been doing a fine job on that front all by themselves. But gay marriage clearly presupposes and reinforces deinstitutionalization.

By itself, the "conservative case" for gay marriage might be attractive. It would be gratifying to extend the benefits of marriage to same-sex couples—if gay marriage and marriage renewal somehow fit together. But they do not. As individuals and as a society, we can strive to maintain and strengthen marriage as a primary social institution and society's best welfare plan for children (some would say for men and women too). Or we can strive to implement same-sex marriage. But unless we are prepared to tear down with one hand what we are building up with the other, we cannot do both.

"In a world where gay couples look married, act married, talk married, raise kids together, . . . the best way to preserve marriage's normative status is to bring gay couples inside the tent."

Same-Sex Marriage Bans Are a Threat to All Nontraditional Families

Jonathan Rauch

In the following viewpoint, Jonathan Rauch maintains that bans on same-sex marriage will only hurt the institution of marriage itself. He disputes the argument that the purpose of a marriage is simply to procreate and argues that a marriage—whether it's between two heterosexuals or two people of the same sex— should provide a stable and healthy environment for children. Rauch, the author of Gay Marriage: Why It Is Good for Gays, Good for Straights, and Good for America, *is a contributing editor of* National Journal *and the* Atlantic.

As you read, consider the following questions:

1. As Rauch relates, what principle does David Blakenhorn claim same-sex marriage denies?

Jonathan Rauch, "Family Reunion: The Case Against the Case Against Gay Marriage," www.DemocracyJournal.org, Summer 2007. Reproduced by permission.

2. In Rauch's view, what are the four essential purposes of marriage?

3. According to the author, what else do people in countries with same-sex marriage tend to be more supportive of than do people in countries without same-sex marriage?

When I came out with a book making the case for same-sex marriage a few years ago, I expected to spend time selling gay marriage to straight people and marriage to gay people. The surprise was how much time I spent selling marriage to straight people.

By marriage, I mean not just a commitment that two people make to each other. Marriage is a commitment that the two spouses also make to their community. They promise to look after each other and their children so society won't have to; in exchange, society deems them a family and provides an assortment of privileges, obligations, and care giving tools. (Not, mostly, "benefits.") Marriage does much more than ratify relationships, I would tell audiences; it fortifies relationships by embedding them in a dense web of social expectations. That is why marriage, with or without children, is a win-win deal, strengthening individuals, families, and communities all at the same time. Gay marriage, I said, would be the same positive-sum transaction. The example gay couples set by marrying instead of shacking up might even strengthen marriage itself.

Audiences received my gay-marriage pitch in predictably varied ways. What consistently surprised me, however, was how few people thought of marriage as anything more than a private contract. Particularly among groups of younger people, the standard view was that marriage is just an individual lifestyle choice. If chosen, great. If not chosen, great. I would leave such encounters with a troubling thought: Perhaps

straights were becoming receptive to gay marriage partly because they had devalued marriage itself.

In his new book, *The Future of Marriage*, David Blankenhorn begins where my doubts left off. Blankenhorn is the
founder and president of his own think tank, the Institute for
American Values, and has built his career on the restoration of
fatherhood to the center of American family life. In *The Future of Marriage*, he emerges as an articulate, humane, and
fair-minded opponent of same-sex marriage, which he regards
as nothing less than part of an effort to steal children's patri-
mony. "It would require us, legally and formally, to withdraw
marriage's greatest promise to the child—the promise that, in-
sofar as society can make it possible, I will be loved and raised
by the mother and father who made me." He takes jabs at me,
among other gay-marriage advocates, but in my case he plays
fair. And Blankenhorn is ambitious. He wants to lift the gay-
marriage debate from its isolation in the mud pit of the parti-
san culture wars and place it within a larger theory of marriage. He also wants to put an end to the days when gay-
marriage advocates can say that there is no serious case against
gay marriage. In both respects, he succeeds.

As I read, I made note of points on which he and I agree.
I soon found myself running out of paper. Marriage, we both
believe, is a vital institution, not just equal to competing family arrangements from society's point of view but preferable; it
is an institution embedded in society, not a mere contract between individuals; it is social, not just legal, and so cannot be
twisted like a pretzel by court order; it has (almost) everywhere and always been heterosexual and entwined with procreation, and should be. Gay marriage, we both believe, is a
significant change that entails risk (though we assess the risks
very differently); but gay marriage, we also believe, is a supporting character in the much larger drama of shifting social
values. We agree that heterosexuals, not homosexuals, will determine marriage's fate and have handled matrimony pretty

poorly without any gay help. And we agree that children, on average (please note the qualifier), do best when raised by their biological mother and father, though he makes more sweeping claims on that score than I would.

That is a great deal of common ground, which makes it all the more interesting that we come out in utterly different places and that gay marriage, in some ways, turns out to be the least of our disagreements.

Gay Marriage Helps to Preserve the Institution of Marriage

For Blankenhorn, "the most important trend affecting marriage in America" is not same-sex marriage. It is the "deinstitutionalization" of marriage—that is, "the belief that marriage is exclusively a private relationship"—which gay marriage is merely a prominent offshoot. To his credit, he understands and forthrightly acknowledges that the individualistic view of marriage "has deep roots in our society and has been growing for decades, propagated overwhelmingly by heterosexuals."

Marriage creates kin. In society's eyes, it distinguishes a relationship from a family. The trouble, for Blankenhorn, with declaring any old kind of relationship a family—with turning marriage into "a pretty label for a private relationship"—is that marriage evolved and exists for a specific social reason, which is to bind both parents, especially fathers, to their biological children. Same-sex marriage, he argues, denies this principle, because its "deep logic" is that a family is whatever we say it is, and it changes the meaning of marriage "*for everyone*" (his italics). For support, he draws on the writings of left-wing activists and academics who favor same-sex marriage precisely because, they hope, it would knock mom-dad-child marriage off its pedestal. Granting marriage rights to gay couples, who even in principle cannot unite biological fathers and mothers with their children, would "require us in both law and culture to deny the double origin of the child." Once that happens, we "transform marriage once and for all from a pro-child social institution into a post-institutional private relationship."

In plainer English, Blankenhorn is saying that marriage is designed to discriminate in favor of conjugal families and must continue to do so. Egalitarians may hate that idea, but it isn't stupid or bigoted. Blankenhorn is correct to think society has a strong interest in keeping fathers, mothers, and children together; many of today's problems of crime, poverty, and inequality flow directly from the breakdown of families. But there Blankenhorn and I part ways. He says he is all for maintaining the dignity and equality of gay people, but he believes that changing marriage's most venerable boundary is the wrong way to do so. I am all for maintaining the strength of marriage and family, but I think that telling homosexuals (and their kids) they can't form legal families is the wrong way to do so.

Having written a whole book on the subject, I won't rehearse here why I think gay marriage is good family policy. Suffice it to say that, in a society riddled with divorce and fatherlessness, family policy's essential task is to shore up marriage's status as a norm. In a world where gay couples look married, act married, talk married, raise kids together, and are increasingly accepted as married, the best way to preserve marriage's normative status is to bring gay couples inside the tent. Failing to do so, over time, will tar marriage as discriminatory, legitimize cohabitation and other kinds of non-marriage, and turn every successful gay couple into a cultural advertisement for the expendability of matrimony.

Blankenhorn clearly disagrees. Our disagreement over how gay marriage will affect marriage's normative status, however, is well-plowed ground. So I'll move along to what Blankenhorn rightly considers his deeper and more important arguments, which are about the nature of marriage itself. Near the beginning of his book, Blankenhorn calls child-rearing (by which he means the rearing of children by their biological parents) "probably the single most important social need that marriage is designed to meet, but there are numerous others as well." Two pages later, however, he makes a more unequivocal statement: "Without children, marriage as an institution makes little sense." Though he regularly uses qualifiers, it quickly becomes clear that, in practice, the unqualified statement is much closer to his view.

Blankenhorn succeeds in showing that binding fathers and mothers to their biological children is a core purpose of marriage, and more power to him for that. But the logic of his argument is that binding fathers and mothers to their biological children is the *only* purpose that has any compelling claim on society, and that allowing marriage to serve any other purpose hurts children by pushing them to the sidelines. From *a* purpose to *the* purpose is a long leap, and one that leaves the public far behind. Blankenhorn himself cites a poll showing that 13 percent of Americans say "promot[ing] the happiness and well-being of the married individuals" is the "more important characteristic of a good marriage," and 10 percent choose "produces children who are well-adjusted and who will become good citizens," but three-quarters say: "The two are about equally important." In other words, the public believes that a good marriage is good for adults *and* good for children, and that there is no conflict.

Infertility Should Not Bar a Couple from Marrying

And the public is obviously right. Marriage has more than one essential public purpose. Providing a healthy and secure environment for the rearing of children (biological or adoptive) is certainly one of them (and, of course, many gay couples are raising children), but at least three others, in my view, compel respect: providing a transition to stable domestic life for young adults (especially men), providing a safe harbor for sex, and providing lifelong caregivers.

Still others can be found in a 2000 document called "The Marriage Movement: A Statement of Principles." In a section headed "What Is Marriage?" the manifesto declares that "marriage has at least six important dimensions": it is a legal contract, a financial partnership, a sacred promise, a sexual union, a personal bond, and a family-making bond. "In all these ways," the statement continues, "marriage is a productive institution, not a consumer good."

That manifesto, as you may have guessed, was drafted, endorsed, and disseminated by David Blankenhorn, among others. The Blankenhorn of 2000 was right. Marriage multitasks. It is undoubtedly linked with procreation, but the reductionist Blankenhorn of 2007 gets the relationship backward: Marriage binds children to parents by conditioning procreation on marriage, not by conditioning marriage on procreation. We regard the marriage of infertile (say, elderly) couples as cause for celebration, not condemnation. And, of course, gay couples are just another variety of infertile couple. Even if their unions do not accomplish all the public purposes of marriage, three out of four—or five out of six—ain't chicken feed.

Blankenhorn, oddly, treats the objection that society values and encourages infertile straight marriages as no objection at all. His three flippant pages explaining why infertility would bar gay but not straight couples from matrimony are the only really embarrassing performance in his book. He says that allowing infertile straight couples to marry no more shows that marriage isn't for biological parenting than allowing nondrivers to buy cars shows that cars aren't for driving. He fails to note that marriage is more like a mobile home (some people drive them, some live in them, and some do both), that it is in fact legal for nondrivers to own cars, and that in any case gay couples are already out on the roads by the thousands. He says barring infertile straight couples would be impractical, as if that were the reason we don't do it. (And, actually, it would be pretty easy; in fact, a satirical Washington State initiative

The Concept of Marriage Has Evolved Over Time

Marriage has undergone many changes to evolve with society, even making dramatic changes in the last century. For example, marriage was not considered a religious institution prior to 1215 when the Catholic Church recognized the union as a sacrament. Also, for centuries, marriage was regarded first and foremost as an economic relationship, a means by which a man obtained property by securing a wife. Not until industrialization did couples marry for love, rather than survival.

"Marriage Arguments,"
OutFront Minnesota, 2012. www.outfront.org.

campaign proposes to do it.) Then, backing up, he acknowledges that practicality isn't the issue, only to tumble headlong into a baffling non sequitur by saying *"there is no need!"* (his emphasis) for a ban on infertile straight marriages because fertile couples will have babies anyway.

In the midst of those pratfalls, he loses this whopper: "Marriage's main purpose is to make sure that any child born has two responsible parents, a mother and a father who are committed to the child and committed to each other. To achieve this goal, *it has never been necessary*, and it would never be possible, *for society to require that each and every married couple bear a child*" (italics mine). Well, thanks. I rest my case.

Those Who Support Gay Marriage Tend to Be More Tolerant

Fortunately, Blankenhorn has a stronger argument to make—although in the end it lands him on the horns of another false dilemma. Setting aside the structure of marriage, he considers the structure of support for gay marriage. It is no coincidence, he says, that "*people who professionally dislike marriage almost always favor gay marriage*" (his italics). Marriage's opponents want to de-privilege marriage, replacing it with a "family diversity" model in which society and law view all family structures as equal and interchangeable. Such folks favor gay marriage, he argues, because they understand it as a step along their downhill path.

Blankenhorn here elides [omits] the fact that many egalitarian anti-marriage activists have expressed ambivalence or outright hostility toward same-sex marriage, precisely because they fear it would undercut their liberationist agenda. He also elides the fact that some of the country's most distinguished and dedicated marriage advocates support same-sex marriage: Paul Amato, William Doherty, William Galston, and Theodora Ooms, among others. He does not explain why a bunch of left-wingers who he and I would probably agree are wrong about almost everything else should be presumed right about same-sex marriage.

Still, Blankenhorn is making a deeper point, and one with an element of truth. He is saying that certain values go together in coherent bundles. If we could have the status quo plus gay marriage, he could live with that. But he thinks we will either get less than gay marriage or much more, because we must choose between two bundles of values, one that puts children at the center of marriage and another that gives primacy to adults. To clinch the point, Blankenhorn draws on two multinational public-opinion surveys. He considers eight questions about marriage, such as "Married people are happier," "People who want children should marry," and "Marriage is an outdated institution." Countries that recognize gay marriage, he finds, are consistently less likely to insist on the importance of marriage than are countries that do not recognize it.

Blankenhorn is saying that only one of these two cultural bundles can sustain marriage as a child-centered public institution. But it is the whole bundle, not just gay marriage, that determines marriage's fate. With exemplary integrity, Blankenhorn acknowledges as much. "To the degree that it makes any sense to oppose gay marriage, it makes sense *only* if one also opposes with equal clarity and intensity the other main trends pushing our society toward post-institutional marriage" (his italics). So the important question isn't only gay marriage, or even marriage. Just as important is what else is in these bundles.

Here is one clue. Countries in his data set that recognize same-sex marriage nationally are relatively few and are concentrated in Western Europe, plus Canada and South Africa. Countries that do not recognize same-sex unions, on the other hand, form a larger and more heterogeneous group, including a few Western countries, but also, for instance, Bangladesh, China, Egypt, Indonesia, Iran, Saudi Arabia, Nigeria, Uganda, and Ukraine. It would certainly be surprising if the latter countries did not take a more traditional view of marriage—and very much else.

And so they do. Using data from the World Values Survey—the larger and, as we both agree, more representative of Blankenhorn's two sources—I looked at how countries with and without same-sex marriage felt on some matters other than marriage. As Blankenhorn points out, countries without same-sex marriage do indeed take more traditional attitudes toward marriage, parenthood, and divorce. But—prepare to be shocked—what correlates most starkly with the absence of gay marriage is intolerance of homosexuals. Meanwhile, people in countries with same-sex marriage are more supportive of teaching children to be independent and tolerant; they are more supportive of women's equality in work and politics; and they are less insistent that women must be mothers to be fulfilled. They are also more secular and are marginally more supportive of democracy. As it turns out, they also report higher satisfaction with life and feel they have more freedom of choice and control over their lives. If you had to live in a random country chosen from one of these two lists, which list would you choose? As a homosexual American, I can tell you my own answer, and not just because of gay marriage.

Blankenhorn has painted himself into a corner, one where the American public will never join him. If, as he insists, we cannot sustainably mix and match values and policies—combine adult individualism with devoted parenthood, for example, or conjoin same-sex marriage with measures to reduce divorce—then we must choose whether to move in the direction of the Netherlands or Saudi Arabia. I have no doubt which way the public would go. And should.

In fact, however, the public will reject the choice Blankenhorn offers as a false one; and, again, the public will be right. A look at Blankenhorn's own data shows that the public of gay-marriage countries have not rejected marriage; on six out of the eight questions he uses as indicators, they agree with non-gay-marriage countries, just by less decisive margins. People in countries recognizing same-sex unions are more accepting of cohabitation and single parenthood than Blankenhorn and I would prefer; but their project is not to reject marriage, except perhaps on Blankenhorn's reductionist account of it, but to blend and balance it with other values of liberal individualism.

Blankenhorn may think this project futile. He is right to sound cautionary notes. But in recent years, as he points out, U.S. divorce rates have dropped a little and teen-pregnancy rates have dropped a lot, while "rates of marital happiness have stabilized and may be increasing." States are experimenting with reforms to strengthen marriage and reduce unnecessary divorce, and the proportion of African-American children living in two-parent, married-couple homes has stabilized or increased. Those modest but heartening improvements come at precisely the time when gay Americans in the millions—the ordinary folks, not the academicians—have discovered and embraced marriage and family after years of alienation from both.

Blankenhorn and I could argue all day about whether gay marriage is part of the solution or part of the problem. But I feel I have learned a couple of things recently. From giving all those speeches, I have learned that the public takes a more individualistic view of marriage than either Blankenhorn or I would prefer. From his new book, I've learned that the public's view of both marriage and society is nonetheless richer, wiser, and more humane than David Blankenhorn's—and possibly, for that matter, than my own, which gives me hope that, whatever the experts say the real purpose of marriage is or is not, the public can ultimately get it right.

> *"For a federal judge to also see that families come in all shapes and sizes and to recognize the unfair impact of marriage discrimination on children's lives is very affirming."*

Children of Gay Parents Support Legalized Gay Marriage

Sarah Wildman

In the following viewpoint, Sarah Wildman contends that the children of gay and lesbian couples strongly support their parents' fight to gain the right to legally marry. She argues that the support that these children show for their parents undermines critics' arguments about the negative effects of gay parents on children. Wildman writes about the connection between politics and culture as well as immigration and citizenship in both Europe and the United States.

As you read, consider the following questions:

1. According to the viewpoint, what is COLAGE?

2. In the author's view, what important point does Judge Walker make in his decision about Proposition 8 and "the gender of a child's parent"?

Sarah Wildman, "Gay Marriage's Biggest Supporters: Children of Gay Parents," Politics daily.com, August 12, 2010. Copyright © 2010 AOL Inc. Reproduced by permission.

3. According to Wildman, in which state was the ban against same-sex marriage overturned?

By now we've all seen (and, in my case, wept over) the images: couples long denied the right to marry swept up in the energy and excitement of a battle (temporarily) won.

With the majority of Americans now polling (for the first time!) in favor of gay marriage, today [August 12, 2010] Judge Vaughn Walker indicated gay marriages will once again go forward, starting August 18, in California. The move came in the wake of last week's Proposition 8 decision, in which Judge Walker ruled the state's ban on gay marriage was unconstitutional. "Proposition 8," Walker wrote, "fails to advance any rational basis in singling out gay men and lesbians for denial of a marriage license."

Amen.

Amid the celebration, the decision was understood by all parties not to be the final word on gay marriage in the state, and certainly not in the country, but nevertheless a cause for great optimism. Those who are most optimistic may not be the couples themselves. A whole population is affected by this decision, a quieter, (sometimes physically) smaller population, and one that has become increasingly political over the last decade. Their stake in the marriage debate, whether they are gay or straight, is one much more fundamental than that of "allies" or friendly supporters.

The Children of Gay Families Need to Know That Their Families Matter

I am speaking, of course, of the children of the gay men and lesbians who hope to marry, the children of those who hope to lift the discrimination levied on their families—homes where two women love one another, or two men. "As a person raised by lesbian moms and gay dads, I am thrilled that the Prop 8 decision recognizes the overwhelming evidence that

LGBT [lesbian, gay, bisexual, and transgender] parents are capable of making households just as loving, nurturing and stable as heterosexual parents," Danielle Silber, the New York City chapter president of COLAGE, e-mailed me Wednesday [August 11, 2010]. COLAGE bills itself as "a national movement of children, youth, and adults with one or more lesbian, gay, bisexual, transgender and/or queer (LGBTQ) parent/s."

Danielle was in Provincetown, Mass., last week, with 300 COLAGE families, when the decision came down. Joy surely rippled up Commercial Street when California's judge announced it. (In the early part of this decade, for years, I spent a week each summer in that bastion of tolerance and wonder, traveling with my closest friend. To me, in that week, the world felt like a more just place.) The executive director of COLAGE, Beth Teper, e-mailed me from her vacation to describe the scene.

> For many children of LGBTQ parents, having a family that's treated differently and discriminated against can be isolating or challenging. But when we meet others who can appreciate that experience because they've been there, we feel seen, heard, and understood—often for the first time. Meeting other young people like ourselves, from families like our own, helps us understand that there are others who know what it's like, and that we're not the only ones and our difference is in fact our strength. For a federal judge to also see that families come in all shapes and sizes and to recognize the unfair impact of marriage discrimination on children's lives is very affirming. Only two hours after Proposition 8 was overturned, nearly two hundred COLAGE supporters gathered at a reception to celebrate both Judge Walker's decision and the organization's 20th anniversary. Jubilant cheers and joyous hoots and hollers were readily heard when the news was announced; hugs and high fives were exchanged among youth and parents alike in acknowledgment of this milestone moment in our families' march toward equality and justice.

Gay Families Produce Happy and Well-Adjusted Children

Whether you've noticed them or not, the children of gay unions were in the picture all along. Opponents of same-sex marriage have long suggested that same-sex marriage will have negative consequences for children of gay parents. Yet, as Judge Walker pointed out, the presence of thriving children in such households provides a dramatic counterpoint.

> Proposition 8 singles out gays and lesbians and legitimates their unequal treatment. Proposition 8 perpetuates the stereotype that gays and lesbians are incapable of forming long-term loving relationships and that gays and lesbians are not good parents.
>
> The gender of a child's parent is not a factor in a child's adjustment. The sexual orientation of an individual does not determine whether that individual can be a good parent. Children raised by gay or lesbian parents are as likely as children raised by heterosexual parents to be healthy, successful and well-adjusted.

Back in December [2009] and January [2010] I interviewed a number of children and adult offspring of gay men and lesbians across the country—some had become increasingly outspoken advocates, loquacious and political. Some, the younger ones, especially, just saw the whole thing as clearly, patently, unfair. The right to wed "means to me that two different people who are in love get to be married or be able to live together legally forever and have special protection rights for the family," McKinley BarbouRoske told me when I was reporting that story. McKinley, a middle schooler, is a regular at gay marriage rallies. Her family was a part of the Iowa lawsuit that overturned that state's ban against same-sex marriage. Of her decision to speak out, McKinley told me: "I decided to do it because, of course, my family and [because] I know there are a lot of other people with families out there who need the freedom for this and I'm trying to do it so everyone has an equal right." In Iowa the children signed on to the case as co-plaintiffs. It was a strategy that worked well to combat those on the opposite side: claiming that "protecting" marriage was on behalf of the children. Lambda Legal, arguing for the gay and lesbian couples, argued that if the argument addressed the children—the real, live children should be involved. Not just in Iowa, either. Across the country, children from lesbian- and gay-headed households have been catapulted from appendices in the conversation about gay marriage into increasingly visible, and key, roles as spokespersons in the debate. The civil rights organizations that support gay marriage have begun to recognize the next generation's potential for changing the terms of the debate. That's what happened when 14-year-old Sam Putnam-Ripley, a Portland, Maine, high school freshman took the floor to testify before Maine's statehouse last August. His five-minute political action, conceived around his kitchen table, immediately attracted the attention of the organizers of "No on 1," the Maine gay rights group that fought the anti-marriage ballot proposal there. Activists approached Putnam's telegenic family and put them in a soft-focus ad campaign. Sitting on a wood front porch surrounded by trees swaying in dappled sunlight, Sam, flanked by his moms, tells the camera, "We can't be seen as lesser." The hope was to have a repeat of the wildly successful Massachusetts equality ad from 2003 highlighting a hockey star—Peter Hams—and his two hockey moms. Hams, muscular and handsome, looks at the camera and says, "I think it's wrong to vote on other people's rights." That television spot was credited by gay rights activists with helping to sway many in Massachusetts.

As Sam told me on the phone, "I hadn't comprehended the impact of my story. I have always loved having two moms. I always thought we were a normal family—I thought there were a lot of families like mine." He hoped, he said, that his "story might be inspiring to other kids to come out and be more open."

Now that we know that kids from lesbian homes actually do better than their peers (or at least have fewer behavior problems), maybe we can all start to look to LGBTQ families as inspirational rather than controversial.

"'This is just what our family does,' says Debra, looking around the room at her children. 'Who would have the right to take this away from us?'"

Same-Sex Partners and Parents Deserve the Same Legal Rights as Straight Couples

Judith Davidoff

In the following viewpoint, Judith Davidoff asserts that banning same-sex marriages and civil unions threatens the ability of gays and lesbians to offer their partners and children such benefits as health insurance, protection against domestic violence, and Social Security payments. She states that such threats cause gay and lesbian couples to worry that their relationships and right to be parents will be legally challenged. Davidoff reports on social issues for the Capital Times *in Madison, Wisconsin.*

Judith Davidoff, "No Wedding Bells," *The Progressive*, vol. 70, no. 8, August 2006, pp. 22–25. Copyright © Progressive Incorporated, August 2006. Reproduced by permission of the author.

As you read, consider the following questions:

1. In Davidoff's opinion, what is affected when civil unions are banned and the ability of the government and private companies to offer domestic partnership benefits is challenged?

2. What did attorney Jay Kaplan refer to as "a bait and switch" in Michigan?

3. According to Eric Peterson, why are religious organizations protesting bans on same-sex marriage and civil unions?

Ray Vahey and Richard Taylor met in Ohio in 1956. Taylor, a World War II veteran, was managing a toy warehouse in Cleveland. Vahey, just out of high school, was in town for the Labor Day weekend. They fell in love the evening they met.

"It was the height of the busy season and he had to work," Vahey recalls. "He taught me how to use a ticket pricer. It was an unusual honeymoon, but it was romantic to me."

The couple has been together ever since, moving around the country as Vahey climbed the corporate ladder. Their sprawling Victorian-style apartment in Milwaukee is stuffed with art and antiques, a shared passion that started when they lived in San Francisco. They've seen each other through major life events, including serious illnesses for them both.

Gay Couples Are Not Able to Take Care of Each Other Without Marriage

But despite their fifty-year commitment, they still don't have access to the routine benefits accorded married couples.

"If one of us dies, the survivor has no right to the other's Social Security payments," Vahey says. "When I retired from my last firm, I could not take an option to cover Richard under my pension, as others could to cover their spouses." And Vahey has no claim to Taylor's veteran's benefits.

They estimate they've spent $10,000 in legal fees to care for each other in sickness and in health, and to make provisions in case of death. But they, and thousands of other gay and lesbian couples across the country, are worried that far-reaching constitutional bans on gay marriage and civil unions on the November [2006] ballot will nullify their stop-gap safeguards.

Since 1998, nineteen states have passed constitutional bans on same-sex marriage, though Nebraska's and Georgia's were struck down and are under appeal. Alabama became the most recent state to pass a ban, with more than 80 percent of voters approving a constitutional amendment in early June.

This fall, voters in Wisconsin and at least five other states will weigh in on whether to ban same-sex marriage within their borders. The amendments in Wisconsin, Virginia, South Dakota, South Carolina, and Idaho would either explicitly or implicitly ban civil unions and threaten benefits for domestic partners. A measure in Tennessee is narrower.

There are also efforts under way in Illinois, Colorado, and Arizona to get same-sex marriage bans on the November ballot, though the Illinois measure would only be advisory to its state legislature. (Colorado already has a fall ballot measure that would create a statewide registry for same-sex couples and give them many of the rights and benefits available to married couples, including health insurance, pension coverage, and hospital visitation rights.)

Gay Marriage Bans Affect Children's Well-Being

The most sweeping amendments, if passed, would ban civil unions and allow social conservatives to challenge the ability of governmental entities and private companies to offer domestic partnership benefits. Also in jeopardy, say legal experts, are parenting and real estate agreements, wills, powers of attorney, and other valuable legal documents that gay and lesbian couples are increasingly using to achieve some of the protections automatically provided by marriage.

"We're talking about language that very clearly bans civil unions and very broadly will ban anything and everything that would be a way for couples to protect each other," says Leslie Shear, a law professor at the University of Wisconsin-Madison and co-chair of the school's Family Law Project.

For Vahey and Taylor, that would be a nightmare.

And it would be a nightmare for Aurora Greane, too. Asked what grade she's in, Aurora doesn't have a ready answer.

"I'm in a variety of grades," chirps the seven-and-a-half-year-old, who reads at the third- and fourth-grade level and spells at the second-grade level.

"That's part of the beauty of homeschooling," explains her mother, Debra. "She can learn at whatever level she's at."

Aurora is working on math problems alongside her mom as sun streams through the large windows of the family's new home in Madison, Wisconsin. The family moved to larger quarters to make room for Debra's elderly mom, who will soon be moving in.

Aurora's sister, Rikaela, fourteen, is at the kitchen breakfast bar conjugating verbs for a Spanish class she takes with other homeschoolers. Shana Greane, Debra's partner and the girls' other mom, is at her job as an occupational therapist for the Madison school system.

It is Shana's job—more specifically, the domestic partnership benefit package offered through the school system—that makes this way of life possible for the Greane family. Otherwise, Debra would have to find a job of her own with health benefits and wouldn't have the time, or energy, to homeschool their kids.

"This is just what our family does," says Debra, looking around the room at her children. "Who would have the right to take this away from us?"

In 2004, Republicans rushed thirteen amendments onto state ballots to coincide with the presidential election. They all passed. In Ohio and Michigan, conservatives quickly challenged domestic partnership benefits. In Utah and Ohio, judges have invoked the amendments to deny domestic violence protections for unmarried heterosexual couples.

"In '04, we were the Chicken Littles," says Carrie Evans, state legislative director of the Human Rights Campaign. "Our legal intuition told us the language in these bans was really bad, but we had no evidence. Now we've had actual real-life consequences."

In Michigan, Citizens for the Protection of Marriage repeatedly stated in its literature and in press interviews that a ban on same-sex marriage would not affect domestic partnership benefits.

"This has nothing to do with taking benefits away," Marlene Elwell, campaign director, told *USA Today* on October 15, 2004. "This is about marriage between a man and a woman."

Domestic Partnership Benefits Are Being Threatened

The campaign's communications director was equally adamant. The proposal would have no effect on gay couples, Kristina Hemphill told the *Holland Sentinel*. "This amendment has nothing to do with benefits," she said.

Yet shortly after Michigan's ban passed, Governor Jennifer Granholm pulled domestic partnership benefits from contracts being negotiated for state workers. And Attorney General Mike Cox issued an opinion stating that such benefits for municipal employees could not be renewed in future contracts.

"It's a bait and switch," says Jay Kaplan, an attorney with the ACLU [American Civil Liberties Union] of Michigan, which filed a lawsuit seeking clarification that Michigan's ban does not prohibit domestic partnership benefits offered by

A Majority of Americans Believe That Gays and Lesbians Deserve the Right to Be Married

According to a May 20, 2011, Gallup poll, 53% of Americans believe that same-sex marriages should be legally valid.

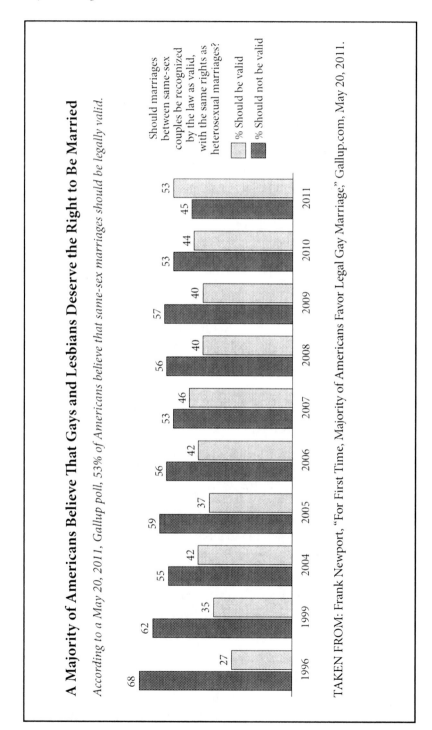

Should marriages between same-sex couples be recognized by the law as valid, with the same rights as heterosexual marriages?

□ % Should be valid
■ % Should not be valid

TAKEN FROM: Frank Newport, "For First Time, Majority of Americans Favor Legal Gay Marriage," Gallup.com, May 20, 2011.

public employers. "They put in ambiguous language because they are trying to roll back other things."

Tom and Dennis Patrick are plaintiffs in the Michigan lawsuit. They rely on domestic partnership benefits offered through Dennis's job at Eastern Michigan University to help raise their children, all of whom joined their family as foster children. (The Patricks have adopted three children and are in the process of adopting a fourth.)

Together for nine years, Tom and Dennis have owned three houses together and now live in an old farmhouse in Ypsilanti. Because Tom, a high school math teacher, is covered under Dennis's health insurance, he can work part-time as a substitute teacher and be at home more often to help with the children, who range in age from four to ten.

This has been particularly important in caring for Joshua, the couple's oldest son, who has epilepsy and has been hospitalized several times because of seizures. Tom's job means he's home every morning before the children leave for school and every afternoon when they return.

"If I were full-time, I'd have to be in the building by 6:45 a.m.," Tom says. "That just didn't work for our family."

Without health care coverage, Tom would face a painful choice: return to work full-time, which would take him away from the kids, or pay for his own insurance, which would impose a huge drain on the household budget. As he puts it, "It would take either money away from our family or time away."

Theresa Roetter, a Madison attorney who specializes in adoption cases, says same-sex couples with children are justifiably worried. She says clients are increasingly turning away from more accepted forms of permanency for children, such as adoption, and accepting legal relationships, like guardianships, in order to have "something they feel will be unassailable" if the constitutional amendment passes.

"What people are looking for is whatever they can get to ensure the child has a legal place in their home," Roetter says.

They are worried that their relationships, even their right to parent, will be "subject to collateral attack in the courts later."

Fair Wisconsin, the main group fighting the ban, has recruited volunteers in each of the state's seventy-two counties to educate people in their own communities about the ramifications of the constitutional amendment.

"We try to emphasize how this will impact real people," says Josh Freker, the group's communications director. "We try to make sure people understand what's potentially at stake with that. We want people to know it would outlaw civil unions and would jeopardize any sort of legal protections for unmarried couples."

Religious Groups Are Helping to Fight the Same-Sex Marriage Bans

Dan Freund is an attorney who practices in Eau Claire, Wisconsin. He volunteered his efforts to help defeat the ban because, as a Unitarian, he feels it is his duty to defend people's civil rights. "My religious faith calls on me to be active in the pursuit of fairness, justice, and equality," he says.

Freund has spoken to more than a dozen civic and religious groups, including the Rotary, Lions, and Kiwanis clubs. He says he's been pleasantly surprised by how receptive many of the groups have been.

Freund said he often tells the story of an Eau Claire woman who was prevented from visiting her longtime partner in a local hospital room because the couple was not considered family.

"They had been together longer than my wife and I," says Freund, who has been married for twenty-four years. If the ban passes, he tells his audiences, the legislature would be prohibited from ever passing a law that would require hospitals to extend visiting privileges to same-sex partners.

Like Freund, many people of faith are taking a stand against the marriage and civil unions ban. The Wisconsin

Conference of the United Church of Christ, representing 241 congregations statewide, opposes it, as does the Wisconsin Conference of the United Methodist [Church], the Wisconsin Jewish Conference, and the Greater Milwaukee Synod of the Evangelical Lutheran Church in America, among others. All told, faith institutions representing nearly 500,000 congregants in Wisconsin publicly oppose this constitutional amendment.

"The ban violates Christian and Jewish values of compassion and fairness," says Eric Peterson, Fair Wisconsin's faith outreach director.

Neither Ray Vahey nor Richard Taylor counted themselves as politically active until the proposed constitutional ban on same-sex marriage. Now Vahey has a table reserved in his study for stuffing envelopes with literature opposing the amendment. And both have testified against the ban at the state capitol.

There, in the state assembly parlor, Vahey and Taylor took note of a large painting depicting the battleship *Wisconsin* under attack by kamikaze pilots during World War II. The scene was familiar to Taylor. After joining the navy at seventeen, he was assigned to a naval tanker on convoy duty in the Mediterranean Sea and North Atlantic and Pacific Oceans.

His tanker, in fact, came under kamikaze attack in the same waters as the battleship *Wisconsin*.

"He valiantly put himself in harm's way to protect his country and all the generations that followed, and now they want to take away his right to justice and equality under the law," Vahey says. "It's ironic, to say the least."

> *"In reality, de facto parenthood serves adults more than children, as it continues adults' liberation from marriage, strengthening their ability to found or join a family however they wish."*

Unmarried Couples Do Not Deserve the Same Parenting Rights as Married Couples

Sara Butler Nardo

In the following viewpoint, Sara Butler Nardo argues that the law should not grant the status of parent to a person without any legal or biological connection to a child. She argues that it discourages and devalues the institution of marriage by artificially creating bonds where none exist naturally. Nardo is a research associate at the Institute for American Values.

As you read, consider the following questions:

1. According to the viewpoint, what does "de facto" or "psychological" parent status mean?

2. As the author reports, what consideration will judges be prioritizing before awarding de facto parenthood rights?

3. What, in the author's view, is wrong with allowing law to create families?

Eleven years ago [1995] Page Britain gave birth to a baby girl, assisted by her partner of six years, Sue Ellen Carvin. Nine months before, Carvin had helped artificially inseminate Britain with sperm donated by a friend. Britain and Carvin raised the little girl together until their relationship ended just before the child's sixth birthday.

Then, Britain tried to prevent Carvin from seeing the child. Carvin went to court, petitioning for visitation rights despite having no legally recognized relationship to the child. In November [2006], the Washington State Supreme Court ruled that Carvin does indeed have legal standing from which to seek visitation. To achieve this result, the court dipped into the magician's hat of common law (loosely defined) and pulled out a rabbit: de facto parenthood.

"De Facto" Parenthood Creates Parents

Washington is only the latest state to embrace this new concept. At least ten states, including California, Maine, Massachusetts, New Jersey, and Wisconsin, allow a person with no legal or biological relationship to a child to petition for "de facto" or "psychological" parent status on the basis of a relationship between the adult and child. The judge can award this legal status if he determines that the adult filled the function of a parent for a sufficient length of time. We are likely to see more courts take this step in the future. As long ago as 2000, the influential American Law Institute issued suggested guidelines for de facto parenthood in its *Principles of the Law of Family Dissolution*, cited in several of the rulings establishing de facto parenthood.

The advent of de facto parenthood has been hailed as a victory for gays and lesbians, who, it is argued, must be allowed to establish legal parenthood this way since they cannot do so through marriage. But judicially created and enforced de facto parenthood is not the only way to address the situation of gay and lesbian couples raising children; indeed, many of the states that have created de facto parenthood already allowed second-parent adoption to gay and lesbian couples, but couples who ended up in court had declined to take advantage of it.

And gays and lesbians are not the only ones seeking de facto parenthood; *Youmans v. Ramos*, one of the cases that defined de facto parenthood in Massachusetts, involved a dispute between 11-year-old Tamika's father and her aunt, who had raised Tamika while her father was away serving in the military. Nor will gays and lesbians be the only ones to suffer from the unintended consequences of creating a new class of parents, retroactively designated and detached from any foundation in biology or adoption.

Under the new regime of de facto parenthood, biological and adoptive parents, gay or straight, may find that they have unintentionally given third-party adults a legally enforceable right to their children after cohabiting or remarrying. The tests that courts have set up to determine de facto parenthood are supposed to take into account the intentions of any legal parents. But will judges really be able to tell whether a mother or father was "fostering a parent-like relationship" between, say, a new lover and a son or daughter or merely encouraging them to get along?

In cases of a subsequent marriage, when the child already has two legal parents, will both parents' attitudes toward their child's relationship with a stepparent be taken into consideration? Or can a parent's access to his or her child be reduced because of a de facto relationship over which he or she had no control? In principle there is no numerical limit to the number of de facto parents a child can have. Custody battles between two parents can get ugly enough—imagine custody battles among three or four.

Marriage Should Not Be Altered for Gays and Lesbians

It is understandable that as a society we should want to address intolerance and discrimination directed toward homosexuals, but it is a profound mistake to attempt to do this by passing laws that fundamentally alter existing social norms and institutions. Whatever the anthropology, social science demonstrates clearly that the needs of children coincide with the received wisdom of the ages articulated in our customs, traditions and, yes, our religions.

Margret Kopala,
"Sacrificing Our Children for Same-Sex 'Marriage,'"
WND.com, May 21, 2008.

While de facto parenthood allows a subsequent spouse or a live-in boyfriend or girlfriend to continue their relationship with a child even after their relationship with the child's legal parent ends, it also allows them to use the threat of suing their ex-partner for de facto parenthood. And there are new potential consequences for parents who invite a family member to live with them. Will grandma want to take her grandchild with her when she moves out?

Biological or Adoptive Parents vs. "Parent-Like"

While the courts have attempted to create objective criteria for de facto parenthood, the category remains far fuzzier than parenthood as traditionally defined. The Washington court, following Wisconsin's model, established a four-part test to be used by judges in determining whether a person has standing as a de facto parent: (1) the natural or legal parent consented to and fostered the parent-like relationship; (2) the petitioner and the child lived together in the same household; (3) the petitioner assumed obligations of parenthood without expectation of financial compensation; and (4) the petitioner has been in a parental role for a length of time sufficient to have established with the child a bonded, dependent relationship parental in nature.

Rather than answering a simple question—Does the adult have a biological or adoptive relationship to the child in question?—judges will award parenthood depending on whether the relationship appears sufficiently "parent-like," a notable expansion of state power in the realm of family life.

The courts have justified the creation of de facto parenthood by arguing it serves the best interests of children. In reality, however, it works at cross-purposes to the institution that most essentially serves children's interests—marriage. Marriage works precisely by binding together the various aspects of parenthood—the biological, legal, and psychological attachments, not to mention the financial and emotional interests, of two parents and their children—which de facto parenthood fragments. In reality, de facto parenthood serves adults more than children, as it continues adults' liberation from marriage, strengthening their ability to found or join a family however they wish, without marrying first, or ever.

This new circular definition of parenthood—a parent is a person who performs the function of a parent—is part of a larger trend in family law that sees the law as the creator of the family, rather than one of its many custodians. According to the new dispensation, the words we use to describe this most vital social institution—family, mother, father, marriage—do not correspond to natural relationships, but are mere labels that the state is free to apply as it sees fit.

In the case of the label "marriage," the proposed change that is currently in the air has been widely and loudly debated. The legal definition of "parent," meanwhile, is already quietly changing.

> *"The law in many places has failed to keep pace with revolution in assisted reproductive technology, making the process a potentially perilous one for the unwary or the unwise."*

As Surrogacy Becomes More Popular, Legal Problems Proliferate

Mark Hansen

In the following viewpoint, Mark Hansen maintains that legal issues, such as parental rights and insurance coverage, will increase as assisted reproductive technologies, including surrogacy, become more available. He contends that as the courts try to balance the rights of the intended parents with those of the surrogate, this issue will have long-term consequences for gay and lesbian couples hoping to have children. Hansen is a senior writer for the ABA Journal.

As you read, consider the following questions:

1. According to Hansen, why should online surrogacy websites not be used to find a surrogate?

Mark Hansen, "As Surrogacy Becomes More Popular, Legal Problems Proliferate," *ABA Journal*, vol. 97, no. 3, March 2011, pp. 53–57. Copyright © American Bar Association, March 2011. Reproduced by permission.

2. Why do some people think that intended parents should be screened to determine their suitability to be parents through surrogacy?

3. According to the author, what is the difference between a traditional surrogacy and a gestational surrogacy?

Like many couples, R.W.S. and B.C.F. wanted a child of their own. But the couple—in this case two gay men from Minneapolis—had ruled out adoption, which left surrogacy their only viable option.

So the two men did what so many others in their position have done: They turned to the Internet.

On the website of Surrogate Mothers Online, a volunteer-run support group for the surrogacy community, they came across a posting from a Minneapolis-area woman offering her services as a surrogate. Before long, the couple entered into a contract with the surrogate and paid her an undisclosed fee for her services. Through medical science, the woman soon became impregnated with a baby from R.W.S.'s sperm and her own egg.

Nine months later the surrogate gave birth—first, to a healthy baby girl, then to litigation.

At first, everything went smoothly between the new fathers and their surrogate. After the baby girl was born, the surrogate visited the newborn at the men's home, and the nonbiological father proceeded with his plans to adopt the little girl, which was to have included a voluntary termination of the surrogate's parental rights. Then, seemingly out of the blue, about a month after giving birth to the girl, the surrogate—identified in court records only as E.A.G.—showed up unannounced at the couple's front door with her father, young son and another surrogate in tow. She proceeded to tell the two men she had changed her mind about giving up the baby and wanted the girl back.

Sound familiar? Surrogacy first entered the collective public conscience almost 25 years ago when Mary Beth Whitehead reneged on her promise to give up all parental rights to Baby M, the daughter for whom she served as a surrogate for a New Jersey couple.

The Baby M case provoked such an outcry in some quarters over concerns about "baby selling" and the possible exploitation of poor women that a number of states enacted bans on surrogacy.

Such concerns have eased somewhat with the growing acceptance and popularity of in vitro fertilization and other types of assisted reproductive technologies that allow a surrogate to bear and give birth to a child she has no genetic or biological connection to, using embryos created in a lab with donated eggs and sperm.

Those procedures, which have opened the possibility of parenthood to a variety of people who can't have children of their own—single people, people with medical issues or infertility problems, same-sex couples and other nontraditional families—have become the new norm in surrogacy arrangements.

Such advances have helped turn the science of making babies into a $3 billion-a-year industry, according to Harvard Business School professor Debora Spar in her 2006 book, *The Baby Business: How Money, Science, and Politics Drive the Commerce of Conception*. The demand has spawned a proliferation of new businesses, including fertility clinics, surrogacy agencies, and online brokers specializing in matching Indian- or Ukrainian-based surrogates with prospective U.S. parents or U.S.-based surrogates with would-be parents in other parts of the world where surrogacy is illegal.

Lawyers who practice in the surrogacy arena say the Baby M case—as well as the Minnesota case—are the exceptions. Most cases, they insist, go smoothly and according to contract. Surrogacy has become so commonplace, in fact, that a host of bold-faced names from Elton John to Sarah Jessica Parker and Nicole Kidman have all publicly acknowledged using surrogates to birth babies for them. The publicity has helped make the process more acceptable as a viable alternative to childbirth.

But surrogacy also can be a minefield. The industry is largely unregulated. And the law in many places has failed to keep pace with the revolution in assisted reproductive technology, making the process a potentially perilous one for the unwary or the unwise.

Reliable figures on surrogacy are hard to come by. No government agency or private group tracks surrogate births, though estimates range from several hundred to a few thousand per year. By one account, about 22,000 babies have been born through surrogacy in this country since the mid-1970s.

Some practitioners say they suspect the actual number is far higher. San Diego lawyer Theresa M. Erickson, who specializes in third-party reproduction and runs her own surrogacy agency, says her office alone handles about 150 such cases a year. And one of her colleagues on the East Coast does nearly as many.

But as medical science continues to push the envelope forward, making the process of having a baby via methods other than that intended by nature accessible to all, the legal issues are multiplying.

A Crazy Quilt of Laws

The United States, unlike many countries, has no national policies governing assisted reproductive technology, including surrogacy. And state laws vary widely from one state to the next. Several states expressly prohibit it, declaring all such agreements void and unenforceable as a matter of public policy. A few even make it a crime to pay for surrogacy. Other states allow it but restrict its use to married couples or to cases in which at least one of the intended parents has a genetic link to the child. And a handful of states have been very open to the use of reproductive technology and have allowed it to flourish.

But a majority of states, including Minnesota, have no laws directly addressing surrogacy, leaving many such arrangements in legal limbo and raising a number of vexing social, legal and ethical issues involving parenthood, the best interests of children, and the rights of same-sex couples and other nontraditional families for the courts to resolve.

Another big issue when it comes to surrogacy is cost. Done with the help of lawyers, doctors, psychologists, facilitators and other professionals, a surrogacy can cost upwards of $100,000, including medical expenses and health insurance. And questions persist about who is responsible for the bills.

Many health insurance policies specifically exclude maternity coverage for surrogates. And some reserve the right to seek reimbursement from the intended parents for any maternity benefits paid on the surrogate's behalf.

At least 14 states currently require some types of health insurance plans to include coverage of certain infertility services, according to a report by the Center for American Progress, a liberal research group. But in some of those states, the mandate applies only to married couples or to couples who use their own eggs and sperm. And most of the 14 contain language that implicitly excludes coverage for single people and gay, lesbian or transgender couples.

The insurance picture may be changing, however.

Last July, the Wisconsin Supreme Court held that insurance companies doing business in that state may not deny routine pregnancy services to surrogate mothers based solely on the means by which they became pregnant or their reasons for doing so.

In its decision, apparently one of first impression, the Wisconsin court said state law allows an insurer to exclude or limit certain services and procedures, as long as the exclusion or limitation applies to all policyholders. But it doesn't allow insurers to make routine maternity services that are generally covered under its policies unavailable to a specific subgroup of insureds, namely surrogates.

While the ruling applies only to Wisconsin insurers, experts say, the same argument could be made in other states where insurers routinely exclude maternity coverage for women serving as surrogates.

Such harsh economic realities are pushing many would-be parents—like the Minnesota couple—to try to cut corners and go the do-it-yourself route. This pro se mentality—which surrogacy lawyers say is on the rise—most often results in surrogacy agreements that break down, frustrate the parties' intentions and wind up in court, experts say.

R.W.S. and B.C.F.'s legal battle with their surrogate has been going on for almost as long as their daughter, now 3 1/2, has been alive.

After two years of legal wrangling, the matter ended up in a Minneapolis court, where a judge sided with the two men. In 2009 after a 10-day bench trial, the judge held that the two men—and not the surrogate—were the girl's legal and biological parents, and awarded them sole legal and physical custody, saying it was in the child's best interests.

The decision is believed to be the first time a court has held, under the Uniform Parentage Act, that a surrogate is not the mother of a child she gave birth to using her own egg. The Uniform Parentage Act has been adopted by many states, and the Minnesota decision caused a big stir in the reproductive law community.

"The courts, for the most part, are not going to disenfranchise a surrogate who gives birth to her own biological child," says Golden Valley, Minn., lawyer Suzanne Born, who represents the two fathers. "That's where this case departs from the norm."

Last October, an appellate court reversed the trial court's determination of parentage, though it affirmed that part of the lower court's decision awarding R.W.S. sole legal and physical custody of the girl.

Perils of the D.I.Y. Approach

The dispute over the Minnesota girl—while unusual, experts say—also serves as a cautionary tale about the potential perils of do-it-yourself surrogacies in a largely unregulated market, where high costs and a patchwork of conflicting laws are the norm.

Steven H. Snyder, a Maple Grove, Minn., lawyer, chairs the ABA Family Law Section's assisted reproductive technologies committee. He says that, despite tales of woe like the Minnesota case, most surrogacies are problem free. "That evidences what seems to me to be a pretty reliable process," Snyder says.

"Done carefully and correctly, it's a wonderful thing," says New Rochelle, N.Y., lawyer Elizabeth Swire Falker, the so-called Stork Lawyer, who has an adoption and reproductive law practice and provides infertility treatment consulting.

Even if the Minnesota case is an exception, lawyers who practice in this area see more clients going it alone, leaving them to come in and try to clean up when things go awry.

Born, who specializes in adoption and assisted reproduction law, is—like everybody connected with the case—under a gag order. But she says this situation is an example of what not to do when it comes to surrogacy.

"I don't think they realized what they were getting into" until it was too late, she says of her clients.

Because a typical surrogacy can cost between $80,000 and $120,000, some prospective parents try to save money by cutting costs and eliminating the services of an agency—which can add $20,000 or more to the overall tab.

But finding a surrogate online through a mass clearinghouse for surrogates, as R.W.S. and B.C.F. did, is usually not a good idea, experts say, because there is no way to be sure of the qualifications, suitability or reliability of the surrogates who are offering their services there.

A reputable agency, on the other hand, will not only carefully screen and prepare potential surrogates for the process but also manage all of the medical, psychological, legal, financial, insurance and administrative details that go along with such an arrangement.

Of course, not all agencies are created equal.

Anybody with a website, a post office box and a telephone number can open an agency and start accepting clients. Some agencies operate as little more than glorified matchmaking services. Others offer a range of surrogacy-related services and adhere to practice and ethical guidelines promulgated by the American Society for Reproductive Medicine.

The industry has been rocked by several recent scandals. One of the biggest to date was the collapse of SurroGenesis, a Modesto, Calif.-based agency that abruptly closed its doors in March 2009, leaving dozens of pregnant surrogates and expectant parents in the lurch and millions of dollars in client funds unaccounted for.

The collapse of SurroGenesis and an affiliated escrow company that was supposed to be safeguarding client funds has led to a class action lawsuit against company officials and ongoing investigations by the FBI and the U.S. Postal Service. It also prompted the ABA committee Snyder heads to begin drafting model legislation to regulate the industry, though that effort is still a work in progress.

Steps to Consider

Snyder and other lawyers who specialize in adoption and surrogacy law say they're not necessarily opposed to working with a client who wants to arrange his or her own surrogacy, as long as the client fully understands and is willing to accept the risks that come with it. But there are certain steps in the process that should be followed even if no agency is involved, they say.

One is a thorough screening of the surrogate and a complete disclosure of life facts and circumstances between the parties. Such a screening serves to educate the surrogate on relevant issues and evaluate her ability to complete the process as intended. A criminal background check, thorough medical history and analysis of any available insurance coverage should also be undertaken.

Some experts recommend that the intended parents also be screened, which could identify issues that might prevent the surrogate from keeping her end of the bargain: a history of mental illness, a criminal record, or evidence of domestic violence or child abuse. But others don't believe the intended parents should be subject to any screening since parents who are capable of having their own children aren't subjected to any screening beforehand.

Born says she has nothing against Surrogate Mothers Online, the information and support group that operates the website where her clients found their surrogate. Her chief concern is that nobody there is evaluating the women who advertise their services as surrogates, which might have revealed that E.A.G. would end up changing her mind.

Kymberli Barney, a mother of four who moderates a discussion list for Surrogate Mothers Online and once served as a surrogate, says there are definite advantages to working with a reputable agency. But, she argues, an agency is not always necessary. "In truth, there isn't anything an agency can do for an individual that the individual can't do for himself," she says.

R.W.S. and B.C.F.'s second big mistake, Born and other experts say, was to agree to a traditional surrogacy arrangement with a woman they didn't know and to whom they weren't related. Though a traditional surrogacy (defined as one where the surrogate is also the biological mother) is simpler and less expensive than a gestational surrogacy (where the surrogate has no biological ties to the child she is carrying), it presents a much greater legal risk for the intended parent(s) if the surrogate changes her mind.

"A woman who gives birth to a child using her own egg is legally presumed to be the child's mother wherever she is," says Nidhi Desai, a Chicago lawyer who specializes in adoption and reproductive technologies.

That's why many lawyers who do such cases for a living are reluctant to get involved in a traditional surrogacy unless the parties are closely related or good friends and know exactly what they're getting into. Some practitioners say they won't handle a traditional surrogacy arrangement under any circumstances.

"I wouldn't touch one with a 10-foot pole," says Falker, the New York lawyer.

Even Barney concedes that it takes a certain frame of mind to serve as a traditional surrogate, one she doesn't happen to have. "I view anybody born from my egg to be my child, so that's not something I would be able to do," she says.

R.W.S. and B.C.F.'s third big mistake, according to lawyers in the field, was to enter into a surrogacy agreement in a state like Minnesota, where the legality of such an arrangement is uncertain, without any input or advice from a lawyer who knows the lay of the land.

The same goes for the Minnesota surrogate, who also should have been represented by competent, independent legal counsel to help ensure that she—and her husband, if she were married—understood and appreciated all of the issues set forth in the agreement and was proceeding with the arrangement voluntarily and without any coercion or undue influence.

In Search of a Standard

In an effort to bring order to the current chaos, some experts have called for a uniform federal law governing surrogacy. Such a standard would prevent forum shopping for states with more favorable surrogacy laws—which reduces the bargaining power of individual surrogates; draws prospective parents from all over the country with the promise of easy, risk-free transactions; and allows agencies to get around the most restrictive state laws.

Another option would be to encourage more states to adopt article 8 of the Uniform Parentage Act, which specifically addresses surrogacy agreements. Article 8, which is optional to enacting states, treats a surrogacy agreement, which it calls a "gestational agreement," as a significant legal act that should be approved by a court in a process similar to an adoption proceeding.

Under article 8, a version of which apparently only two states have so far adopted, a court has to verify the birth mother's qualifications to carry a child and the intended parents' qualifications to be parents. It also says that a birth mother may be compensated for her services and has the power to terminate the agreement.

The act also stipulates that surrogacy agreements not approved by a judge are unenforceable, which provides a strong incentive for the parties to seek judicial scrutiny, and that prospective parents who enter into an unapproved surrogacy agreement and then refuse to adopt the resulting child may be liable for child support.

In 2008, the ABA adopted a model act governing assisted reproductive technologies, including surrogacy. The model act, which was 20 years in the making, is designed to provide a flexible framework by which issues such as parentage, informed consent, mental health consultation, privacy and insurance can be approached and resolved.

The model act proposes two alternative ways of handling surrogacy arrangements: One would require a judge's pre-approval of any surrogacy agreement in which neither of the intended parents has a genetic link to the resulting child; the other, an administrative model, would require no judicial involvement as long as at least one of the intended parents has a genetic link to the resulting child and all of the parties submit to eligibility and procedural requirements—including a mental health evaluation, a legal consultation and health insurance coverage.

But the ABA's efforts so far have fared even worse than article 8 of the Uniform Parentage Act has in terms of state legislative acceptance, leaving many such arrangements in legal limbo for the time being.

At the moment, the Minnesota couple, R.W.S. and B.C.F., are still in that limbo, but they currently appear to hold the upper hand. The surrogate appealed the unfavorable court ruling to the Minnesota Supreme Court, which in mid-January denied her petition for further review. And while the surrogate is expected to take her case to federal court, the federal courts generally don't get involved in custody disputes that don't raise diversity or constitutional issues.

And according to court records, the young girl still lives with her two dads, whom she recognizes as her parents, in their Minneapolis home—the only home she has ever known.

Periodical and Internet Sources Bibliography

The following articles have been selected to supplement the diverse views presented in this chapter.

Stephen Baskerville	"The Real Danger of Same-Sex Marriage," *The Family in America*, May/June 2006. www.pro fam.org.
Joan Biskupic	"Same-Sex Couples Redefining Family Law in USA," *USA Today*, February 17, 2003.
Frank Bruni	"One Country's Big Gay Leap," *New York Times*, October 8, 2011.
John Corvino	"Gay Marriage and the 'Bigot' Card," *Humanist*, July/August 2009.
William C. Duncan	"De Facto Parents," *National Review Online*, August 31, 2009. www.nationalreview.com.
Family Research Council	"The Slippery Slope of Same-Sex 'Marriage,'" 2004. www.frc.org.
Nathaniel Frank	"Does the Religious Right Really Care About Children?," *Huffington Post*, October 28, 2011. www.huffingtonpost.com.
Jason Frye	"Stop Saying 'Same-Sex' Marriage," *Humanist*, September/October 2011.
Mark Ira Kaufman	"The Fake Threat of Gay Marriage," *The Mark Ira Kaufman Journal*, March 19, 2011. http:// open.salon.com.
Michael Medved	"NY Gays Tie the Knot: What's Lost by Re-Defining Marriage," Townhall.com.
Thomas Messner	"Religion and Morality in the Same-Sex Marriage Debate," *Backgrounder*, no. 2437, July 20, 2010. www.heritage.org.

For Further Discussion

Chapter 1

1. Walter Schumm, in an interview conducted by LifeSite News.com, argues that research about the impact of gay and lesbian parents on children is biased and inaccurate because of researchers' concerns about being called homophobic. Abbie Goldberg, in an interview by Suzanne Wilson, maintains that such studies are valid, even among a large number of people being studied. Which argument is more persuasive? Why?

2. Michael Medved contends that Lisa Miller should not have to share custody with her former partner, who has no biological connection to her daughter. Do you agree with his arguments? Why or why not? Use information from Medved's viewpoint to support your statements.

Chapter 2

1. After evaluating the first two viewpoints in this chapter, decide whether you think that Michael Alvear's argument that gay families enhance society is stronger than Brian Camenker's argument that they do not. Use information from Alvear's and Camenker's viewpoints to support your answer.

2. Austin R. Nimocks makes his points in his viewpoint by detailing his argument for traditional families without using a personal anecdote. Do you think using a personal point of view would help make the argument for or against gay families stronger? Why?

Chapter 3

1. After evaluating the viewpoints about religion and the rights of homosexuals to adopt and become foster par-

ents, decide whether you think gay men and lesbians are a threat to religious freedom. Justify your opinion with quotes and information from the viewpoints in this chapter.

2. After reading the viewpoints on assisted reproduction in this chapter, do you think that it is necessary for children to know who their biological parents are? Why or why not? Explain your reasoning and use information from Liza Mundy's and Mark Morford's viewpoints to support your answer.

Chapter 4

1. David Blankenhorn maintains that same-sex marriages weaken the concept of marriage while Jonathan Rauch argues that same-sex marriages actually help to strengthen the institution of marriage. Who makes a stronger case? Why?

2. After reading Mark Hansen's viewpoint about the lack of definitive and clear laws regarding assisted reproduction, do you think that states should adopt article 8 of the Uniform Parentage Act, in which a judge must "verify the birth mother's qualifications to carry a child and the intended parents' qualifications to be parents" and in which the birth mother has the right to end the contract and may be compensated? Why or why not? Use information from Hansen's viewpoint to support your opinion.

Organizations to Contact

The editors have compiled the following list of organizations concerned with the issues debated in this book. The descriptions are derived from materials provided by the organizations. All have publications or information available for interested readers. The list was compiled on the date of publication of the present volume; the information provided here may change. Be aware that many organizations take several weeks or longer to respond to inquiries, so allow as much time as possible.

COLAGE

1550 Bryant Street, Suite 830, San Francisco, CA   94103
(415) 861-5437
e-mail: colage@colage.org
website: www.colage.org

COLAGE is composed of the children, teens, and adults who have at least one parent who is gay, lesbian, bisexual, or transgender. The group's mission is to help these families gain acceptance in society. COLAGE's publications include the *Donor Insemination Guide, Kids of Trans Resource Guide, Let's Get This Straight: The Ultimate Handbook for Youth with LGBTQ Parents*, and the newsletter *Just for Us*.

Concerned Women for America (CWA)

1015 Fifteenth Street NW, Suite 1100, Washington, DC   20005
(202) 488-7000 • fax: (202) 488-0806
website: www.cwfa.org

Concerned Women for America (CWA) is a women's organization devoted to public policy issues that protect and promote traditional values through education and legislative action. The CWA supports traditional marriage, abstinence, and religious liberty, as well as opposes abortion, pornography, and sex education. It publishes *Data Digest* and the monthly *Family Voices*.

Family Research Council
801 G Street NW, Washington, DC 20001
(202) 393-2100 • fax: (202) 393-2134
website: www.frc.org

The Family Research Council is devoted to promoting marriage and family. It opposes homosexuality and condom distribution programs in schools and supports abstinence until marriage. The council publishes such research papers and brochures as *Homosexuality Is Not a Civil Right* and *Getting It Straight: What the Research Shows About Homosexuality.*

Institute for American Values/Center for Marriage
and Families
1841 Broadway, Suite 211, New York, NY 10023
(212) 246-3942
e-mail: info@americanvalues.org
website: www.americanvalues.org

The Institute for American Values is dedicated to studying and strengthening civil society. One of its divisions—the Center for Marriage and Families—promotes marriage between a man and a woman and the traditional family as the bedrock of society that must be protected. The center's publications include *Why Marriage Matters, One Parent or Five?: A Global Look at Today's New Intentional Families,* and *My Daddy's Name Is Donor: A New Study of Young Adults Conceived Through Sperm Donation.*

Institute for Marriage and Public Policy (iMAPP)
PO Box 1231, Manassas, VA 20108
(202) 216-9430
e-mail: info@imapp.org
website: www.marriagedebate.com

The Institute for Marriage and Public Policy (iMAPP) is devoted to strengthening marriage as a social institution. iMAPP opposes same-sex marriage and adoption by gay and lesbian couples and studies the effects of no-fault divorce on the rate of divorce. iMAPP's publications include the *Marriage Law Digest,* the *iMAPP Research Brief,* and *Marriage and the Law: A Statement of Principles.*

Lambda Legal
120 Wall Street, 19th Floor, New York, NY   10005
(212) 809-8585
website: www.lambdalegal.org

Lambda Legal is a national organization dedicated to protecting the civil rights of lesbian, gay, bisexual, and transgender (LGBT) people, as well as the rights of those with HIV and AIDS. The group's focus includes protecting the rights of LGBT and HIV-positive people to become parents and representing such individuals in custody cases. Its publications include the monthly online newsletter *In Brief* and *Impact* magazine.

National Center for Lesbian Rights (NCLR)
870 Market Street, Suite 370, San Francisco, CA   94102
(415) 392-6257 • fax: (415) 392-8442
e-mail: info@nclrights.org
website: www.nclrights.org

The National Center for Lesbian Rights (NCLR) is devoted to improving the human and civil rights of lesbian, gay, transgender, and bisexual people and their families. The group's issues include marriage equality, parenting, and protecting other relationships. The NCLR's publications include *Legal Recognition of LGBT Families; Adoption by Lesbian, Gay, and Bisexual Parents: An Overview of Current Law; Lifelines: Documents to Protect You and Your Family;* and the newsletter *On the Docket.*

National Gay and Lesbian Task Force
1325 Massachusetts Avenue NW, Suite 600
Washington, DC   20005
(202) 393-5177 • fax: (202) 393-2241
website: http://thetaskforce.org

The National Gay and Lesbian Task Force works toward increasing equality for gay, lesbian, transgender, and bisexual people. Their issues include helping such individuals become parents—through adoption, donor insemination, surrogacy, or as foster parents. The task force publishes such reports as "Lesbian, Gay, Bisexual and Transgender (LGBT) Parents and Their Children" and such fact sheets as "Why Civil Unions Are Not Enough."

National Organization for Marriage (NOM)
2029 K Street NW, Suite 300, Washington, DC   20006
(888) 894-3604
e-mail: info@nationformarriage.org
website: www.nationformarriage.org

The National Organization for Marriage (NOM) is devoted to preserving traditional marriage. NOM is opposed to same-sex marriage, supports state and local initiatives against same-sex marriage, and works to educate the public about the need for traditional marriage. Its publications include *Marriage Amendments and Same-Sex Union Recognition* and *Why Marriage Matters.*

Parents, Families and Friends of Lesbians and Gays (PFLAG)
1828 L Street NW, Suite 660, Washington, DC   20036
(202) 467-8180 • fax: (202) 349-0788
e-mail: info@pflag.org
website: www.pflag.org

Parents, Families and Friends of Lesbians and Gays (PFLAG) is devoted to helping lesbian, gay, bisexual, and transgender people and their families gain acceptance in all facets of society. PFLAG's issues include helping gays and lesbians become foster and adoptive parents, advocating in gay custody cases, and supporting same-sex marriage initiatives. It publishes newsletters such as *PFLAG Update* and *PFLAGpole*, as well as other resources including *Faith in Our Families: Parents, Families, and Friends Talk About Religion and Homosexuality* and *Opening the Straight Spouses' Closet.*

Bibliography of Books

Harlyn Aizley, ed. *Confessions of the Other Mother: Nonbiological Lesbian Moms Tell All.* Boston, MA: Beacon Press, 2006.

M.V. Lee Badgett *When Gay People Get Married: What Happens When Societies Legalize Same-Sex Marriage.* New York: New York University Press, 2009.

David Blankenhorn *The Future of Marriage.* New York: Encounter Books, 2007.

David M. Brodzinsky and Adam Pertman, eds. *Adoption by Lesbians and Gay Men: A New Dimension in Family Diversity.* New York: Oxford University Press, 2012.

Michael L. Brown *A Queer Thing Happened to America: And What a Long, Strange Trip It's Been.* Concord, NC: EqualTime Books, 2011.

Andrew J. Cherlin *The Marriage-Go-Round: The State of Marriage and the Family in America Today.* New York: Alfred A. Knopf, 2009.

James C. Dobson *Marriage Under Fire: Why We Must Win This War.* Sisters, OR: Multnomah Publishers, 2004.

Abigail Garner *Families Like Mine: Children of Gay Parents Tell It Like It Is.* New York: HarperCollins, 2004.

Abbie E.
Goldberg

Lesbian and Gay Parents and Their Children: Research on the Family Life Cycle. Washington, DC: American Psychological Association, 2010.

Marybeth Hicks

Don't Let the Kids Drink the Kool-Aid: Confronting the Left's Assault on Our Families, Faith, and Freedom. Washington, DC: Regnery Publishing, 2011.

Stephen Hicks

Lesbian, Gay, and Queer Parenting: Families, Intimacies, Genealogies. New York: Palgrave Macmillan, 2011.

Kathleen E. Hull

Same-Sex Marriage: The Cultural Politics of Love and Law. New York: Cambridge University Press, 2006.

Troy Johnson

Family Outing: What Happened When I Found Out That My Mother Was Gay. New York: Arcade Publishing, 2008.

William Stacy
Johnson

A Time to Embrace: Same-Sex Relationships in Religion, Law, and Politics. 2nd ed. Grand Rapids, MI: W.B. Eerdmans Publishing Company, 2012.

Ellen Lewin

Gay Fatherhood: Narratives of Family and Citizenship in America. Chicago, IL: University of Chicago Press, 2009.

Rena M. Lindevaldsen | *Only One Mommy: A Woman's Battle for Her Life, Her Daughter, and Her Freedom: The Lisa Miller Story.* Orlando, FL: New Revolution Publishers, 2011.

Jacquelyne Luce | *Beyond Expectation: Lesbian/Bi/Queer Women and Assisted Conception.* Toronto, Ontario: University of Toronto Press, 2010.

Erwin W. Lutzer | *The Truth About Same-Sex Marriage: 6 Things You Must Know About What's Really at Stake.* Chicago, IL: Moody Publishers, 2010.

Laura Mamo | *Queering Reproduction: Achieving Pregnancy in the Age of Technoscience.* Durham, NC: Duke University Press, 2007.

Susan Gluck Mezey | *Gay Families and the Courts: The Quest for Equal Rights.* Lanham, MD: Rowman & Littlefield Publishers, 2009.

Mignon R. Moore | *Invisible Families: Gay Identities, Relationships, and Motherhood Among Black Women.* Berkeley, CA: University of California Press, 2011.

Gary Mucciaroni | *Same Sex, Different Politics: Success and Failure in the Struggles Over Gay Rights.* Chicago, IL: University of Chicago Press, 2008.

Martha C. Nussbaum — *From Disgust to Humanity: Sexual Orientation and Constitutional Law.* New York: Oxford University Press, 2010.

Nancy D. Polikoff — *Beyond Straight and Gay Marriage: Valuing All Families Under the Law.* Boston, MA: Beacon Press, 2008.

Jonathan Rauch — *Gay Marriage: Why It Is Good for Gays, Good for Straights, and Good for America.* New York: Times Books, 2004.

David Rayside — *Queer Inclusions, Continental Divisions: Public Recognition of Sexual Diversity in Canada and the United States.* Toronto, Ontario: University of Toronto Press, 2008.

Kimberly D. Richman — *Courting Change: Queer Parents, Judges, and the Transformation of American Family Law.* New York: New York University Press, 2009.

Craig A. Rimmerman and Clyde Wilcox, eds. — *The Politics of Same-Sex Marriage.* Chicago, IL: University of Chicago Press, 2007.

Alan Sears and Craig Osten — *The Homosexual Agenda: Exposing the Principal Threat to Religious Freedom Today.* Nashville, TN: Broadman & Holman Publishers, 2003.

Brette McWhorter Sember
Gay & Lesbian Parenting Choices: From Adoptions or Using a Surrogate to Choosing the Perfect Father. Pompton Plains, NJ: Career Press, 2006.

Louis P. Sheldon
The Agenda: The Homosexual Plan to Change America. Lake Mary, FL: FrontLine, 2005.

Judith Stacey
Unhitched: Love, Marriage, and Family Values from West Hollywood to Western China. New York: New York University Press, 2011.

Glenn T. Stanton and Bill Maier
Marriage on Trial: The Case Against Same-Sex Marriage and Parenting. Downers Grove, IL: InterVarsity Press, 2004.

Mark Strasser
Same-Sex Unions Across the United States. Durham, NC: Carolina Academic Press, 2011.

Fiona Tasker and Jerry J. Bigner, eds.
Gay and Lesbian Parenting: New Directions. New York: Haworth Press, 2008.

Yvette Taylor
Lesbian and Gay Parenting: Securing Social and Educational Capital. New York: Palgrave Macmillan, 2009.

Frank Turek
Correct, Not Politically Correct: How Same-Sex Marriage Hurts Everyone. Charlotte, NC: CrossExamined, 2008.

| Ludger H. Viefhues-Bailey | *Between a Man and a Woman?: Why Conservatives Oppose Same-Sex Marriage.* New York: Columbia University Press, 2010. |
| Lynn D. Wardle, ed. | *What's the Harm?: Does Legalizing Same-Sex Marriage Really Harm Individuals, Families or Society?* Lanham, MD: University Press of America, 2008. |

Index